The Art of Style

The Art of Style

How to Become a Fashion Icon

Illustrated with Over 200 Colorful Images

Laura Merano

Coquille Dorée

ISBN: 978-83-971997-3-6

Fashion has become unfashionable.
Style never.
Coco Chanel

Table of Contents

Introduction

Welcome to a journey through fashion where timeless elegance meets modern individuality. This book is your guide to discovering the transformative power of personal style, inspired by the lives and looks of some of the most iconic women in history. From legendary Hollywood stars to contemporary fashion mavens, these women have influenced trends and carved out unique identities that resonate across generations.

In an era where fashion is more accessible and diverse than ever, finding your style can feel both exhilarating and daunting. With countless trends flooding our social media feeds and fashion magazines, it is easy to lose sight of what truly speaks to you. This book aims to simplify that journey by providing you with the tools and inspiration to uncover and cultivate a style that is authentically yours.

We will examine eight styles that have played a significant role in classic elegance and how they can be interpreted in modern times. We will also delve into the stories of women who have left an indelible mark on the fashion world. From the classic sophistication of Audrey Hepburn, Grace Kelly, Wallis Simpson, and Jacqueline Kennedy to the bold and avant-garde choices of Marlene Dietrich, Elsa Schiaparelli, Lauren Bacall, and Diana Vreeland, these icons offer valuable lessons on embracing who you are through what you wear.

But this book is not just about looking back. It is about looking within. Your style is a reflection of your personality, values, and experiences. It is an ever-evolving expression of who you are and who you aspire to be. By understanding the elements that make up a signature style, you will learn to curate a wardrobe that complements your body and aligns with your lifestyle and aspirations.

Throughout these pages, you will find practical advice on building a versatile wardrobe, tips on selecting pieces that flatter your figure, and insights into developing a cohesive look that stands the test of time. We will explore how to fusion classic elements with modern trends, ensuring your style is timeless and current.

Moreover, this book will encourage you to embrace the experimental side of fashion. Finding your style is as much about trying new things as it is about understanding your preferences. Whether you are a seasoned fashion enthusiast or someone just beginning to explore the world of style, this book is here to inspire and guide you. The journey to discovering your style is deeply personal and incredibly empowering.

So, let's embark on this stylish adventure together. Let the stories of these remarkable women ignite your passion for fashion, and let their timeless elegance and bold choices inspire you to find and embrace your unique style.

Laura Merano

I.

Defining Style:
From Elegance Icons to Personal Identity

What Makes a Style Icon?

A style icon is an individual whose fashion choices and personal style resonate profoundly with people, influencing trends and inspiring admiration across generations. These individuals often transcend their primary professions—be it acting, modeling, or royalty—by establishing a lasting impact on the fashion world. Their style is not just about what they wear, but how they carry themselves, their charisma, and their ability to communicate identity and personality through clothing. Let's explore what makes a style icon through the examples of several remarkable women.

Timeless Elegance

One of the hallmarks of a style icon is timeless elegance. Carla Bruni-Sarkozy, former First Lady of France, embodies this quality with her sophisticated and polished look. Whether in tailored suits or elegant dresses, her preference for classic silhouettes and neutral colors creates a refined and enduring aesthetic that continues to inspire. Bruni-Sarkozy's fashion choices reflect a deep understanding of subtlety and grace, making her a perpetual source of style inspiration.

Revolutionary Approach

Style icons often revolutionize fashion norms and introduce new aesthetics. Coco Chanel, for instance, transformed women's fashion in the 20th century by introducing simplicity and comfort. Her iconic creations, such as the little black dress and tweed suits, remain staples in modern wardrobes, showcasing her lasting influence. Chanel's revolutionary vision redefined femininity and liberated women from restrictive clothing, paving the way for contemporary fashion.

Boldness and Modernity

Icons of style also bring a sense of boldness and modernity. Louise Brooks, with her sleek bob haircut and flapper dresses, epitomized the liberated spirit of the 1920s. Her daring fashion choices and androgynous charm set her apart and continue to inspire contemporary fashion. Brooks' influence can be seen in the ongoing popularity of short haircuts and flapper-inspired designs, highlighting her impact on modern aesthetics.

Cultural Influence

The ability to influence culture through fashion is another defining trait of a style icon. Diana, Princess of Wales, not only captivated the world with her royal elegance but also used her fashion choices to convey messages of empathy and solidarity. Her humanitarian work and thoughtful wardrobe selections showcased her commitment to important causes, further enhancing her iconic status. Diana's style continues to be emulated, reflecting her enduring cultural impact.

Versatility and Adaptability

Versatility and adaptability are crucial for a style icon. Audrey Hepburn's evolution from classic Hollywood glamour to a minimalist, elegant style demonstrated her ability to remain relevant across different eras. Her iconic looks, such as the little black dress in "Breakfast at Tiffany's," continue to be emulated by fashion enthusiasts today. Hepburn's lasting appeal comes from her ability to switch styles while keeping her unique charm.

Innovative Design

Innovative design and a unique vision are essential for those who influence fashion on a broader scale. Elsa Schiaparelli, with her surrealist designs and bold use of color, pushed the boundaries of fashion in the early 20th century. Her creative approach and collaboration with artists like Salvador Dalí cemented her place as a pioneering figure in the fashion industry. Schiaparelli's avant-garde creations inspire modern designers, showcasing her lasting legacy.

Charismatic Presence

A charismatic presence and the ability to make a statement through fashion are key elements of a style icon. Jacqueline Kennedy Onassis, with her impeccable taste and graceful demeanor, defined American elegance in the 1960s. Her stylish outfits, including the famous pillbox hats and

13

tailored suits, set trends that are still celebrated today. Onassis' fashion legacy endures, influencing generations of women to embrace sophistication and poise.

Enduring Influence

The enduring influence of a style icon is seen in how their fashion choices continue to inspire and resonate. Catherine, the Princess of Wales, exemplifies this with her elegant and relatable style. Her thoughtful wardrobe selections, often blending high street and designer pieces, have made her a modern fashion icon admired by many. Catherine's ability to connect with people through her style underscores the timeless appeal of simplicity and elegance.

Innovation and Impact

Icons like Sheikha Moza bint Nasser shape the fashion industry with their innovative vision and impactful presence. Sheikha Moza's sophisticated and modern approach to traditional attire has made her a global fashion icon. Her ability to seamlessly blend cultural heritage with contemporary design sets her apart as a visionary leader in fashion.

In essence, a style icon is someone who leaves an indelible mark on the fashion world through their unique sense of style, innovative approach, and charismatic presence. They inspire generations, challenge conventions, and set trends that stand the test of time. Whether through timeless elegance, revolutionary design, or cultural influence, these icons shape how we perceive and engage with fashion.

The Importance of Having a Personal Style

Having a personal style is more than just following the latest fashion trends. It is about expressing individuality and confidence. For women, cultivating a unique style offers numerous benefits beyond mere aesthetics.

Self-Expression

The personal style allows women to express their personalities, values, and emotions through clothing. Just as Diana Vreeland used her distinctive taste to make bold fashion statements, every woman can use her wardrobe to convey who she is and what she stands for. This self-expression can boost confidence and help women feel more authentic.

Empowerment

A well-defined personal style could be incredibly empowering. When a woman knew what she liked and felt good in her clothes, she projected confidence and self-assurance. This empowerment was evident in icons like Lauren Bacall, whose sophisticated and professional wardrobe complemented her persona as a respected actress, reinforcing her authority and credibility.

Consistency and Recognition

Having a consistent style can make a woman more recognizable and memorable. Just as Victoria Beckham's sleek and polished aesthetic has become synonymous with her brand, women can create a lasting impression through a cohesive wardrobe that focuses on their unique tastes and preferences.

Practicality and Efficiency

Developing a personal style can also make shopping and dressing more efficient. By understanding what works for her body type, lifestyle, and preferences, a woman can build a versatile and functional wardrobe.

Adaptability

A personal style does not mean being rigid or unchanging. It can evolve, reflecting different stages of life, experiences, and personal growth. Icons like Rania al-Abd Allah, Queen of Jordan, demonstrate how personal style can adapt while maintaining an essence that reflects cultural respect.

Economic Sense

Investing in timeless pieces that define style can be more economical in the long run. Instead of constantly chasing fleeting trends, women can focus on high-quality, versatile items that offer longevity and can be mixed and matched effortlessly. This approach promotes sustainability.

Inspiration and Influence

A unique personal style can inspire others and create a positive impact. Carolina Herrera has shown how personal style can influence broader fashion trends and empower other women to embrace their unique looks.

Cultivating a personal style is a powerful tool for women. It enhances self-expression, boosts confidence, and provides practical benefits in daily life. By embracing their individuality through fashion, women can make lasting impressions, feel more empowered, and inspire others.

II.

Cultivating Taste:

The Journey to Personal Style

Taste, Flavor, and Style

These three concepts always go hand in hand. Although seemingly associated with the visual realm, that is, what pleases the eye, they encompass a part of reality. Taste, regarded as an aesthetic preference, is a characteristic admired in individuals who stand out for their elegance not only in their attire and surrounding themselves with beautiful objects, but also in reading books, listening to music, watching movies, and pursuing hobbies. Sense of flavor is interpreted as understanding the rules governing aesthetics. Although, like taste, it also applies to non-material things. Note that flavor is reminiscent of culinary taste (as it is in many European languages). Similarities can be observed: a dish may not taste good to us – just as the beauty of an object or part of clothing, the content of a book and movie, the style of music, or the manner of spending free time may not "taste" good.

From both concepts, we are very close to style. Having taste (or a sense of flavor) makes it easier to develop an individual style resistant to fads and devoid of superficiality.

Why is it worth discussing tastes?

In defining the concept of taste, we often point to the sense of beauty, elegance, harmony, and aesthetics. We are aware that it is not given to everyone. Each of us can identify someone in our surroundings who is valued for their sense of taste and set an example. We can also set out examples of people whom we believe lack taste.

The Latin maxim "de gustibus non est disputandum" refers to the sense of beauty, suggesting that tastes should not be disputed. Is it so? Every mature person wishing to be considered a free thinker has the right to express their views – especially since reality does not always pamper our eyes with harmony and elegance. It is not about openly criticizing others for their misguided choices (as such behavior contradicts the concept of good manners), but about observing, drawing conclusions, and becoming sensitive to beauty.

We are not born with a refined taste. We shape it throughout our lives and can mold and work on it. It is very empowering, as history knows cases of women who have developed a sense of taste to such an extent that they have transformed from individuals prone to fashion and image-related mistakes into style icons.

Factors Influencing Taste Perception

Shaping taste requires knowledge. It broadens awareness and teaches us to perceive the surrounding reality sensibly. With this knowledge, we make more responsible choices and can assess what holds value and what is merely external glitter.

Taste suggests various choices to us – not only in clothing and accessories but also in the books we read, the movies we watch, and the music we listen to. It guides us on how to fix our homes, what architecture we prefer, and how we should spend our free time. It indicates which passions to develop and what topics to discuss. Without a developed sense of taste, it is impossible to imagine a modern woman, conscious of her choices and preferences.

Many factors influence taste perception. An essential role – perhaps even the most crucial – is played by the environment in which we live and grow up. We often carry good examples from our family home. Growing up among people who show us what style and taste are, we have a better chance of drawing from those resources as adults. However, most of us go through adolescent rebellion, manifesting – usually with the help of clothing and hairstyle – a negative attitude towards classicism and tradition. This tendency usually fades after a few years, but it is valuable because it brings experience.

Taste perception is also influenced by the environment in which we operate. People we encounter on our path play a significant role: at work, at university, among friends and family. Role models provide us with inspiration for changes, broaden our horizons, and ignite new interests.

They can encourage us to change our style, discover new passions, and adopt a different perspective on reality.

Taste is also shaped by what we feed our souls – the movies and TV shows we watch, the books we read, and the social media profiles we follow. We should approach all these sources with caution because they can be superficial. Media messages geared towards commercial success, shallow content, and loud opinions of celebrities are not always indicative of good taste – despite receiving applause from millions of viewers.

The audience in cinemas or in front of the television cannot suggest that a film or program is high quality. The fact that a particular book is available in every bookstore indicates that it is well-promoted by a team of marketing experts, not necessarily that it is genuinely good. The number of followers on Instagram is a testament to popularity, not necessarily good taste. Therefore, let us not succumb to manipulation in our judgments but rely on our sensibility – even if they are unpopular choices.

How to Shape Taste

Since taste perception can be developed and we are not born with a formed taste, let's consider how we can do it. Below are four methods to help shape it.

Firstly: Collect Experiences.

Since a similar principle applies to taste perception as when eating, remember the rule of trying. If you don't taste a dish, you won't know if you like it. The same goes for clothing, literature, entertainment, or company. A significant path to shaping taste is collecting experiences, trying, and experimenting. Even if you make a failed clothing purchase, a mismatched hairstyle, read a dull book, or have a lousy evening in a terrible environment, you will probably avoid similar elements next time. No one is infallible, and everyone has made misguided choices – even the most elegant lady, admired for her excellent taste. Success lies in experiencing and drawing the right conclusions, and taste perception is shaped through trial and error.

Secondly: Expand Knowledge.

The more knowledge we have about a given subject, the easier it is to assess its value. So, expand your knowledge to determine whether a particular element belongs to the high or row end. By reading high-quality literature, you will quickly realize the difference between noble writing and books for a less ambitious audience. Watching good movies will show you how different they are from shallow ones with predictable stories. By listening to many genres of music, you'll realize which composer creates at a higher level. By browsing fashion magazines from different eras – not just the latest ones but also the past century – you'll know whether the current trend is fresh or harks back to a historically known style. Therefore, gather information and show interest in various phenomena. With this knowledge, you'll see the wide range of possibilities available. You'll then make a more informed choice.

Thirdly: Nourish the Soul with Beauty.

The contemporary world offers us so many possibilities in clothing, entertainment, and cultural offerings that it is sometimes challenging to discern what is worthy of attention in this chaos. Beauty intertwines with unattractiveness, which tries to aspire to beauty. To form your opinion about the value of certain elements, it is worth nourishing the soul with what is considered the canon. Helpful are good publishers, cultural institutions, and places where beauty is gathered. Therefore, visit museums, look at art albums, and spend time in beautiful interiors. Don't avoid entertainment seemingly reserved for a narrow audience: even if you don't fall in love with opera and become a fan of contemporary art, you'll form your own opinion about such entertainment. Additionally, thanks to modern technology, you don't have to leave home to visit the world's most magnificent places: many famous museums and landmarks offer online tours.

Fourthly: Surround Yourself with Interesting People.

Since the environment influences taste formation, it's worth paying attention to who creates it. Try to spend time with fascinating people who inspire you to change. Meet interesting friends who always have something intriguing to say. Conversations with such people can be a motivation for development. If among them, you find someone you can admire for their elegance and taste, observe them: maybe you'll take some element from their lifestyle for yourself. Of course, it's not about blind imitation, as such experiments rarely benefit anyone, but about inspiration filtered through your senses and taste. Remember that the company you keep has a significant influence on you and on shaping your taste.

Ten Places Helpful in Shaping Taste

Many of the world's famous museums offer the opportunity to view their collections online. It is an option for those who want to broaden their horizons without leaving home. Virtual tours of such places enhance sensitivity and open the eyes to various visual forms.

Remember, the more you feed your soul with beauty, the better taste you cultivate. However, getting to know historical works brings even more benefits. It's an opportunity to expand knowledge and a pretext to start a conversation in an elegant company.

Below are links to ten famous museums that allow you to view their exhibits online.

The British Museum, London
https://britishmuseum.withgoogle.com/

Museo Reina Sosia, Madrid
https://artsandculture.google.com/partner/museo-reina-sofia?hl=en

Uffizi Gallery, Firenze

https://artsandculture.google.com/partner/uffizi-gallery?hl=en%C2%BB

Louvre, Paris

https://www.louvre.fr/en/online-tours

The Metropolitan Museum of Art, New York

https://artsandculture.google.com/partner/the-metropolitan-museum-of-art

Musée d'Orsay, Paris

https://artsandculture.google.com/partner/musee-dorsay-paris?hl=en

National Gallery of Art, Washington

https://artsandculture.google.com/partner/national-gallery-of-art-washington-dc?hl=en%C2%BB

Pinacoteka di Brera, Milan

https://artsandculture.google.com/entity/pinacoteca-di-brera/m0b2_mh?hl=en

Rijksmuseum, Amsterdam

https://artsandculture.google.com/partner/rijksmuseum

Van Gogh Museum, Amsterdam

https://artsandculture.google.com/partner/van-gogh-museum?hl=en

Illustrations from the Art Deco Era

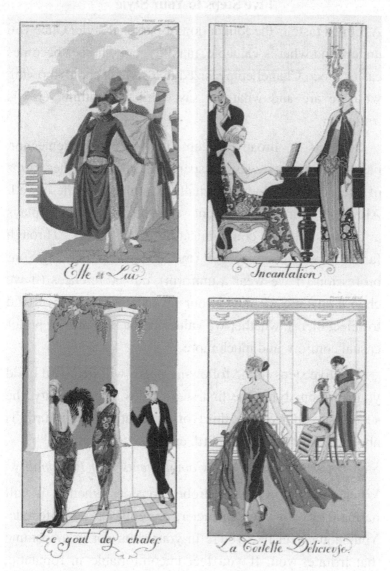

Viewing historical works of art sensitizes us, sparks the imagination, and provides knowledge of classic fashion styles. Above are drawings by the famous French illustrator George Barbier, who, with exquisite artistic sensitivity, captured the wardrobe of the Art Deco era.

Five Steps to Your Style

A refined taste is the foundation of personal style. Once you understand what is valuable, making good choices becomes easier. Coco Chanel emphasized that style is about knowing who we are and what we say, while everything else is irrelevant.

Style is a broad concept that includes demeanor, passions, interests, ways of spending time, and other forms of life activity. Clothing usually complements these well. Although attire is only one element of style, it plays a crucial role in communicating with others. Through fashion, we can convey a lot (metaphorically speaking): our profession (if we wear a uniform), our preferences (if we choose specific garments), our favorite colors (as we tend to select them), whether we value classic elegance or prefer casual comfort, and much more.

The five steps in the following pages will help you build your fashion style. The first step relates to personality, the second to choice, the third offers caution, the fourth is about confidence, and the fifth emphasizes lightness.

Step 1: Choose a Style that Complements Your Personality.

When selecting your wardrobe, consider whether it will harmonize with your character, preferences, and lifestyle. You should feel like you're in your skin, not in a costume that irritates you. If you feel uncomfortable in romantic, flowing dresses, choose clothing from a different category: simple cuts, minimalist forms, and more structured designs. If you feel uneasy in body-hugging clothes, choose looser, more movement-friendly pieces. Don't mindlessly follow foreign patterns (from fashion magazines or the internet) or mimic the style of other women, even if they look amazing. Look to stylish women for inspiration and consider borrowing selected elements of their style.

At this stage, answer these questions:

- In what outfits do I feel confident?
- What clothing provides me with comfort and freedom?
- What type of wardrobe suits my personality and lifestyle?

Step 2: Focus on Elements that Enhance Your Beauty.

As you work on your style, remember not to become a slave to fashion. Trends change so rapidly that it's hard to keep up. Not all trends are equally successful (some are fleeting fads of a single season), some distort the female silhouette, and others look unattractive. Notice that exceptionally stylish women not only stick to certain clothing solutions for years but also always stay a step behind fashion. If a particular dress cut highlights their figure's strengths, they don't abandon it after one season just because new trends emerge. If pastels flatter them, they don't adopt neon colors in vogue for the season, knowing those shades don't align with their style. So, choose only what is best for your type of beauty. Avoid clothes that detract from your appearance, clash with your silhouette, age you, or make your image look gloomy.

At this stage, ask yourself:

- In which outfits do I look youthful and joyful?

- Which clothing colors add radiance to my appearance?
- Which cuts of clothing accentuate my figure's strengths?

Step 3: Don't Strive for Originality.

Does having your style mean you must spectacularly stand out from others? Does it mean you must shine and be noticeable from a hundred meters away? Not. Seeking an individual style is not about forcefully searching for originality. Such tendencies often lead to eccentricity, which doesn't benefit any woman. Notice that historical style icons (Brigitte Bardot, Audrey Hepburn, Grace Kelly, Jacqueline Kennedy Onassis) never forced originality at all costs. They chose understated clothing that highlighted their natural beauty and adhered to all rules of elegance. They understood that forcing originality often skirts the line of good taste. Remember, style is about coherence, not eccentricity.

Ask yourself:

- Is my way of dressing coherent?
- Is the clothing I choose not too eccentric and unusual, maintaining the rules of elegance and good taste?
- Am I avoiding the trap of seeking originality at all costs?

Step 4: Make Confidence an Integral Part of Your Style.

Even the most elegant outfit won't impress without the personality to back it up. Therefore, it's important to confidently present the style you've chosen. Confidence should come not only from self-belief but also from the conviction that you look great in your chosen clothing.

Fashion in Old Portraits

Visiting museums broadens one's horizons. Viewing the exhibits (including paintings) provides insight into the history of clothing. Above are four portraits where one can admire the craftsmanship of historical tailors and jewelers: the Marquise of Chasseloup-Laubat (1) by Joseph-Désiré Court from 1831, Pauline Bonaparte (2) by François Kinson from 1808, Auguste Amalie Prinzessin von Bayern, Duchess of Leuchtenberg (3) by Joseph Karl Stieler from 1825, and a woman (4) by Miklós Barabás from 1831.

If you look in the mirror and are satisfied with your appearance, you will likely project this confidence to those who see you in that outfit. Conversely, if you believe a particular style doesn't suit you, this will show in your posture, glances, walk, and gestures. Lack of self-belief will be evident in your nonverbal behavior. So, remember to add a solid dose of confidence to every outfit.

Ask yourself:

- Am I confident that I look good in my chosen style?
- Am I satisfied with how I present myself?
- Do I have enough self-confidence?

Step 5: Embrace Lightness and Effortlessness

Style doesn't benefit from rigidity and forced effort. Nor does it gain charm from a panic over making mistakes. When choosing your wardrobe, let yourself be guided by lightness. Appreciate effortlessness. Don't become too stiff when presenting yourself in a dignified or elegant outfit. Wanting to look good and dignified doesn't mean you have to seem constrained by your clothing. Try not to look like you spent hours in front of the mirror perfecting your outfit. Don't take clothing too literally: enrich your ensemble with a relaxed element, roll up your sleeves, unbutton the top button, tie a scarf jauntily, or pin an interesting brooch on your jacket lapel. Italians, renowned for their style, use the term "sprezzatura," which means lightness and has become synonymous with classic elegance with a touch of nonchalance. Embrace effortlessness and allow yourself a bit of freedom in your approach to styling.

Illustrations from the 19th Century

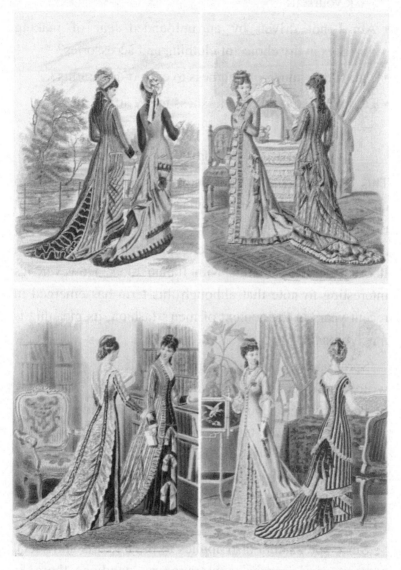

Famous museums have collections of prints featuring historical fashion. The illustrations above are drawings from the 19th-century French fashion magazine Les Modes Parisiennes. The prints are from issues of the magazine published in 1878 and are part of the collection at the Rijksmuseum in Amsterdam.

Ask yourself:

- Am I not driven by an unfounded fear of making mistakes in my choice of clothing and accessories?
- Can I add a touch of lightness to each of my outfits?
- Do I allow myself effortlessness in my attire?

Sprezzatura – Italian Ease of Dressing

This concept, synonymous with an effortless approach to conventions, has gained popularity in recent years about male elegance. It appears where classicism is enriched with a touch of nonchalance and deliberate carelessness in attire. It often describes outfits with Italian roots. However, it's interesting to note that although this term has emerged in recent years in the context of men's fashion, its meaning is much broader.

Sprezzatura was first described in 1528 by the Italian writer and diplomat Baldassare Castiglione in "The Book of the Courtier." During the Baroque period, the term was used to draw attention to the overly rigid approach of artists to conventions in music, painting, literature, and architecture. Sprezzatura is also a concept in social manners. It signifies subtle nonchalance in behavior and a lightness in approaching difficult situations.

Since sprezzatura also applies to the fine arts and social customs and serves contemporary dandies, there is no reason not to use the term to describe feminine elegance.

Fashion in the Museum

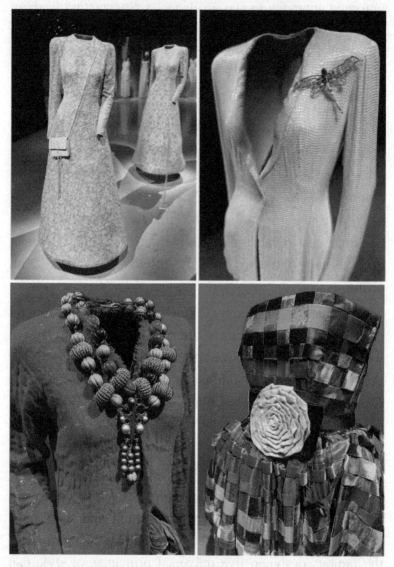

Outfits created by renowned fashion designers are featured not only in exhibitions but also in museums. The photos above show exhibits collected at the Armani/Silos museum in Milan. This institution allows visitors to admire the garments by the Italian designer Giorgio Armani.

It can be found where we see ease in dressing style and an unforced approach to classic elegance. Sprezzatura is about avoiding literalness, clothing references from other eras (adapted to modern requirements), grace in dressing, and a non-imposing form.

Principles of Style by Coco Chanel

One of the most renowned fashion designers in history had a keen sense of trends and revolutionized the approach to clothing. Gabrielle Bonheur Chanel (1883-1971), known as Coco, was not afraid of solutions that were very modern for her time. She opted for simplified cuts and almost ascetic decorations, contrasting with the fashion of the early 20th century.

The creations crafted by Chanel aligned with the societal changes occurring in Europe after World War I. Progressive women boldly emphasized their independence with the help of comfortable outfits in simple silhouettes. The Chanel-style wardrobe harmonized with a dynamic lifestyle, encouraging activity (professional, recreational, and sporting) and suggesting that the woman who wore it was familiar with emancipation.

Coco Chanel's style is considered timeless. However, her garments and her views on fashion and chic have entered the canon of elegance. Reflecting on the opinions of the famous designer, five universal principles of style can be defined.

Coco Chanel Style

Fashion is not something that exists in dresses only.
Fashion is in the sky, in the street, fashion has to do
with ideas, the way we live, what is happening.

Coco Chanel

Principle 1: Dress, Don't Disguise.

It's hard not to notice that many contemporary fashion creations do not meet the needs of attire or clothing suitable for the "street." Eccentric outfits and imaginative forms often do not leave the catwalks or fit into everyday situations. Sometimes, such garments distort the silhouette, dangerously border on kitsch, or even expose the wearers to ridicule. Although fashion aspires to be called art, according to Chanel's view, if you can't wear it on the street, it shouldn't be called fashion. The renowned designer suggested that the utility of clothing was crucial, not the originality bordering on good taste, reminiscent of a costume.

Tip for You: Before reaching for something unusual presented at fashion shows and in fashion magazines, think about how you will look in this outfit.

Fashion passes, style remains.

Coco Chanel

Principle 2: Embrace Timeless Classicism.

The famous designer believed that clothing with a classic form and high quality does not become outdated at the end of the season. Timelessness is synonymous with classicism – not only in fashion. Classicism is often a hallmark of true style. Chanel suggested that women should invest in a standard wardrobe, such as a modest black dress with a non-avant-garde cut, and create a base from it. Assuming they will reach for it for at least several seasons, she advised changing its character and enriching it with accessories (jewelry, shoes, bags, hats). Formulated by the designer many years ago, this idea fits perfectly with the modern approach to clothing. Nowadays, there is much talk about not buying items for just one season (because it's unethical and uneconomical) but rather investing in durable items and opting for vintage pieces. Interestingly, many Chanel designs from years past have not aged at all.

Tip for You: Avoid buying clothing items not to do with classicism and good style if you suspect they will end up at the bottom of your closet.

I want to dress active women, and an active woman has to feel comfortable in her clothes.

Coco Chanel

Principle 3: Pursue Elegance in Comfortable Attire.

Comfort is an element of feeling good in a particular outfit. It was important for the famous French designer because she was an incredibly active woman herself. She understood the need for comfort in other women. She created many clothing classics that didn't restrict movement, were suitable for work, and allowed outdoor recreation. She suggested soft blazer-like jackets, which are now associated with her style. She sewed simple wide trousers. She shortened the pre-World War I maxi length, offering skirts and dresses in a comfortable and chic midi version. She was the first to use soft jersey, which until then had only been used as lingerie fabric. She looked at the outfits of fishermen, which inspired her to dress women in simple navy and white striped tops.

Tip for You: Remember that elegance does not exclude comfort. Therefore, opt for comfortable classics in which you feel good and that do not hinder you in fulfilling your daily duties.

Simplicity is the keynote of all true elegance.

Coco Chanel

Principle 4: Appreciate Refined Simplicity.

Coco Chanel was known for subtracting: accessories, decorations, and other embellishments from her creations. She also encouraged her clients to do the same, suggesting that before leaving home, they should critically look in the mirror and remove at least one element: a scarf (if a necklace adorned their neck), a second ring (if one prominent ring already adorned their hand), a third bracelet (since their wrist was trimmed with two others). The famous French designer was dubbed the queen of the poor, not only because she rejected ostentation in appearance but also because she promoted the idea of affordable ready-to-wear clothing and artificial jewelry. She said that luxury is not the opposite of poverty but of vulgarity. She believed that simplicity can be elegant and refined – she was a living example confirming this thesis. For example, she promoted the classic combination of white and black. The latter of the two colors was her favorite. She believed that black is an exceptionally refined color and that every woman looks elegant in it regardless of the situation.

Tip for You: When composing an outfit, pay attention not to overdo it, as elegance is not demonstrated by the abundance of decorations and accessories but rather by their modesty.

A woman who doesn't wear perfume has no future.

Coco Chanel

Principle 5: Pay Attention to Accessories.

According to a famous French designer, good perfumes complement any outfit. The formula of an exclusive and modern fragrance for those times was developed by Ernest Beaux. In mid-1922, the perfumes went on sale under the name Chanel No. 5. They are still popular today, but according to many women, they have an outdated character, and their sales are due to the legend that accompanies them. The designer attached great importance to jewelry (looking at old photographs, one can see that her neck was often adorned with strings of pearls). Although she usually wore jewelry made of natural metals and minerals, she did not shy away from artificial ones. Chanel was the first to propose so-called fashion jewelry, made of metal and imitation precious stones, cheaper and widely available. She knew that accessories determined the final character of an outfit. She emphasized their role and encouraged careful selection.

Tip for You: Remember that accessories are the proverbial icing on the cake when composing a stylization. Inappropriately chosen accessories will nullify your efforts. Well-matched ones will elevate the level of clothing and emphasize elegance.

III.

The Science of Style:
Techniques and Principles

The Art of Matching

When we look at the attention-worthy outfits of various women, we often gaze enviously at the cuts, colors, and wardrobe compositions they wear. We wonder if those styles would suit us as well. Sometimes, the clothing choices of others can fascinate us to the point where we would thoughtlessly wear the same thing. However, this way of thinking harbors a trap.

Not every wardrobe element that looks great on another woman will look equally good on you. This is an old truth proving that blindly following fashion trends and engaging in faithful imitation is not worthwhile. It's also not worth it for another significant reason. The style has nothing to do with mimicry, although – boldly admitted – it often draws from inspirations. When making difficult clothing choices it's worth remembering that perfect people don't exist. We often forget this, getting lost in achieving an ideal appearance, as promoted by photos published on the Internet and adorning the covers of glossy magazines.

What cannot be changed (and perhaps isn't worth it) should be accepted and learned to live in harmony with the less-liked aspects of one's figure. The most important role in one's dressing style is not played by the silhouette but by the ability to choose clothes that accentuate all its strengths.

Optical Illusions in Service of Attire

In composing a wardrobe and crafting one's style (which we can call a clothing code), knowledge of visual rules comes in handy. The optical illusions mentioned can work in our favor. However, improperly applied, they can do more harm than good. Therefore, it's worth understanding how they work. Illusions regarding the perception of colors and sizes play a crucial role.

The skill is hiding what is too large or disproportionate while showcasing what is delicate, graceful, and deserves attention. For example, if your asset is a narrow waist, accentuate it, and no one will notice the extra pounds in the hips. If you have shapely legs, emphasize their presence with garments of appropriate cuts so that attention is not focused on overly broad shoulders.

Skillful use of optical illusions relies on directing others' gaze to accentuated body parts while diverting it from areas we are less proud of. Playing with colors, cuts, and textures can bring many benefits and joy. Experimenting with different wardrobe styles and accessories will help determine what suits you and what attire suits you best and develop your dress code.

Principle 1: Brighter and Bolder

This rule pertains to colors and their saturation. Elements in brighter and bolder colors give the impression of being bigger, more significant, and closer compared to details in darker and muted colors. The most eye-catching components of a composition are those characterized by brighter or bolder shades. Therefore, attention should initially be directed towards elements that stand out in this manner. This rule is particularly evident with black and white, but it also works with combinations of vibrant colors (e.g., yellow, orange, pink, light green) with subdued ones (navy, charcoal, brown). Understanding this principle is available in handy when we want to highlight specific elements while diverting attention from others.

How can you utilize this optical rule?

- If you intend to conceal ample hips wear a dark skirt and a light-colored blouse.

- To divert attention from a sizable bust and accentuate shapely legs, opt for a sweater in a muted color and pants in a vivid hue.

- When aiming to draw attention to the face and away from the silhouette, choose a dark dress in a solid fabric and accessorize with a colorful scarf around the neck.

Optical Illusions

Optical illusions can deceive the eye, which believes that elements in lighter and brighter colors are larger, more important, and closer. In the photos, there are two examples: one is a colorful composition, and the other is black and white. When observing the photographs, we notice that the eye first gravitates towards the white, then captures the planes in vivid shades, and finally focuses on the darkest elements.

The play of light and dark colors: the white shirt takes the lead, pushing the black vest into the background. The shirt competes with the gray hat and colorful patterns on the tie.

Optical Illusions

The light pink outfit in the top photo appears larger than the dark pink dress of the same cut next to it. In the lower photo, the model in a blouse in an intense shade of pink draws attention first, leaving the lady in beige in the background.

Optical Illusions

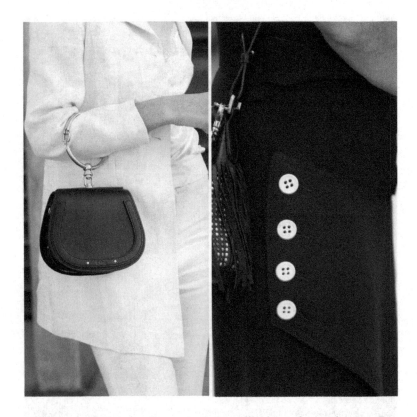

White and black in play, creating an illusion of prominence. In the photo on the left, the broken white outfit of the model stands out, even though the black handbag is a striking element of the styling. In such a combination, the small leather bag may appear even smaller than it is. In the photo on the right, the most noticeable elements are the white buttons, which, against the black background, become so prominent that they overshadow the fringed and silver-decorated handbag.

Optical Illusions

Light colors visually enlarge and broaden, while dark colors shrink and narrow. This rule is illustrated by photos where we see a model in a dress of the same cut in two colors. The light-colored outfit is more visible, highlighting the curves of the figure. The dark-colored attire is less conspicuous and more concealing.

Principle 2: Size and Proximity

This rule is related to the perception of the size of specific elements – depending on the size of others nearby. Small items look even tinier next to larger ones, while large items become more prominent when placed among more petite elements. It's essential to consider proportions. Oversized elements can overwhelm petite figures and may look exaggerated on bigger individuals.

How can you utilize this optical rule?

- If you have a petite frame, opt for shorter and closer-fitting garments. Avoid long, wide, oversized clothing, hefty collars, and large pockets. Choose small bags, sleek headgear, and delicate jewelry. Opt for dainty shoes with slender heels. Avoid oversized tote bags, wide-brimmed hats, and large pendants. Purchase clothing with subtle patterns (small checks, polka dots, and flowers). Avoid big checks and bold geometric and floral patterns.

- If you have a larger or taller stature choose longer, wider, and more flowing clothing. Be cautious with tight and short items. You can indulge in substantial collars, cuffs, pockets, and buttons. Opt for larger-sized bags. Choose footwear with wedges, platforms, and broad heels. Reach for substantial jewelry: massive pendants on long chains, ornate earrings, and broad bracelets. Wide-brimmed hats with a larger crown and wider brim suit you well. Choose fabrics with large geometric and floral designs.

Optical Illusions

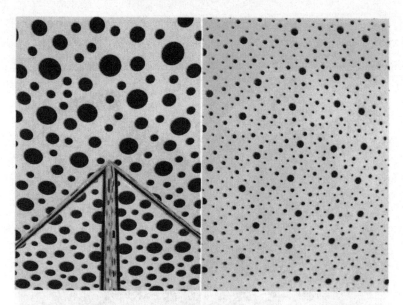

Visual play with patterns, i.e., size perceived through neighboring elements. Small black dots appear even smaller when surrounded by large polka dots. This rule also works the other way around, as large details gain optical weight near smaller elements.

This photo illustrates distorted proportions. The oversized shopping bag draws attention, overshadowing not only the entire outfit but also the model. The large ring also draws attention, competing with the substantial watch. The overall look would be better if the lady chose a sleeker bag and omitted the ring or replaced it with a more delicate one.

Optical Illusions

Inappropriately chosen accessories often disrupt the proportions of the entire outfit. Large accessories can overwhelm and emphasize a petite figure, while small ones can highlight unwanted or expansive features. In the photo on the left, we see a model whose subtle face and slim figure are overshadowed by a hat with too high a crown and too wide a brim. This lady would look better in a smaller headpiece. In the photo on the right, the situation is different. The straight blonde hair and striking facial features of the model would look better in a hat with a wider brim. A larger headpiece would also interestingly complement the dress with a bold pattern.

Optical Illusions

Polka dot fabrics are cheerful and rejuvenating. They are also an interesting motif in a black or white wardrobe if you want to add a touch of playfulness. The size of the polka dots on a blouse, dress, or skirt should match the silhouette. Slimmer ladies can choose outfits with small and medium dots, as the smaller pattern complements their figure. Heavier ladies and those with fuller busts should opt for clothing with larger dots (like the model in the photo on the right). This rule applies also to other patterns: flowers, checks, stripes, and irregular patterns.

Optical Illusions

Visual illusions and the perception of accessory sizes using examples of handbags. In the photo on the left, we can see how the size of a small red bag is diminished against the tall height of the model. The perception is also influenced by the second, shorter lady holding a much larger brown handbag. In the photo on the right, we see a distortion of proportions. A bag of this size would look much better on a taller and sturdier woman – on a petite woman, it is almost grotesque.

Principle 3: Lengthening and Shortening

This rule is associated with perceiving elements arranged vertically and horizontally. Details of the first kind visually elongate, while those of the second kind shorten.

The illusion at play here can distort the perception of a person's height or weight. The lines mentioned create patterns on fabrics (including stripes or details in rows), cuts (i.e., seams and cuts), and accessories (jewelry, shoes, accessories). If these lines are vertical, they optically add height and slimness. If they form horizontally, they visually subtract centimeters and widen.

How can you utilize this optical rule?

• If you want to visually slim down your figure, wear a midi-length dress with vertical stripes, a skirt with prominent seams along its length, or pants with side stripes.

• To emphasize the waist, cinch it with a wide contrasting belt. To visually broaden your shoulders and bust, choose a sweater or blouse with wide stripes. You can visually slim down the upper body with clothing featuring a V-neckline, a long necklace, or a scarf.

• When aiming to highlight the length of your legs, wear stockings in the same color as your skirt or knee-high boots extending at least to the hemline.

Optical Illusions

Optical illusion using architecture in Costa Nova in the Portuguese city of Aveiro. Houses painted with horizontal stripes appear wider than buildings adorned with vertical lines.

Horizontal lines visually widen and shorten, while vertical lines slim and elongate. This principle is especially noticeable in wardrobe elements with striped patterns.

Optical Illusions

Illusions are created not only by traditional stripes but also by planes where various elements form lines. This is visible in fabric patterns. In the photo on the left, there are fabrics with vertical patterns, which visually elongate and slim the silhouette. The picture on the right shows horizontal patterns, which visually widen the silhouette.

Amplified optical illusion, where horizontal stripes on a sweater are reinforced by the horizontally divided plane of the handbag.

Optical Illusions

The photos illustrate the effect of horizontal composition elements. Lines formed by boots and knee-high socks cut across the legs, visually shortening them. The models are saved by having long and slim legs. Women with fuller shapes and thicker legs might look grotesque in such styles.

Before you develop your style

After a detailed analysis of optical illusions that play a significant role in clothing, let's move on to the issue of body types.

On the following pages, you will find descriptions of five body types. Each includes a list of wardrobe items worth considering and those to avoid. Examples are also provided. Items in the first category will help you highlight your assets, while those in the second category will help conceal flaws.

By being aware of the type of clothing that suits you and accentuates your strengths, you can start working on your style. Knowing which cut, color, or fabric looks best on your figure will help you avoid mistakes in choosing clothes and avoid elements that detract from your beauty.

Case 1: X-Silhouette (Typically Feminine)

This figure includes a sizable bust, prominent hips, and a distinct waistline. It is often described as an X-shaped silhouette, due to its resemblance to the letter X. If you possess this type of figure, your goal should be to maintain balance between its upper and lower parts. Therefore, avoid clothing elements that disrupt harmony and create a sense of overwhelm. Opt for lightness and garments that subtly highlight your assets.

Not recommended:

• Blazers and coats with padded shoulders
• Skirts, pants, and dresses made of very thick fabrics
• Very tight trousers
• Wide and long sweaters and turtlenecks
• Pants and skirts with large seat pockets

Recommended:

• Fitted blazers, jackets, and coats
• Blazers and blazers up to the waist
• Blouses and sweaters with a V-neckline
• Wide belts emphasizing the waist
• Long necklaces and scarves

Clothes for X-Silhouette

Case 2: A-Silhouette (Bulky Lower Body Compared to the Upper)

This silhouette, known as type A, is characterized by wide hips and substantial thighs with noticeably slimmer arms and a small bust. To mitigate the disproportion, you should highlight the upper body to draw attention to it. Avoid clothing that accentuates the hips and thighs in favor of attire that highlights the bust and arms.

Not recommended:

- Body-hugging blouses and sweaters in dark colors
- Narrow-cut trousers
- Pencil skirts
- Pants with patterns in intense colors
- Clothing with large seat pockets

Recommended:

- Flowy blouses with bold-colored patterns
- Substantial and expressive necklaces
- Blouses with ties and other decorations at the neckline
- Skirts and dresses with an A-line
- Straight or wider-cut trousers in dark colors

Clothes for A-Silhouette

Case 3: H-Silhouette (Boyish Figure)

Characterized by a lack of a clearly defined waist, this figure, often known as type H, has similar proportions in the upper and lower body - without prominent bust and hip lines. With this silhouette, you should opt for clothing that emphasizes feminine features and accentuates the waist.

Not recommended:

• Blouses tucked into pants

• Clothing items made of stiff fabrics

• Tight and short blouses and sweaters

• Long and trailing skirts with a straight cut

• Pants with wide legs

Recommended:

• Colorful blouses and sweaters with patterns

• Jackets and dresses with breast pockets

• Tunics in colorful designs

• Dresses and skirts that show off the legs

• Blouses and sweaters with a V-neckline

Clothes for H-Silhouette

Case 4: O-Silhouette (Round)

Resembling the shape of the letter O, this figure is often bulky with a poorly defined waist. If you have this type of silhouette, your goal should be to visually elongate and slim it down with the help of appropriate wardrobe tricks.

Not recommended:

• Blouses and dresses in large colorful patterns

• Clothing items in horizontal stripes

• Fitted blouses, sweaters, and jackets

• Tops with thin straps

• Pants in light colors or with patterns

Recommended:

• Blouses and sweaters with a V-neckline

• Flowy tunics in muted patterns

• Dresses with an A-line and a raised waist

• Dark straight-cut trousers

• Skirts and dresses that show off the legs

Clothes for O-Silhouette

Case 5: V-Silhouette (Bulky Upper Body Compared to the Lower)

This silhouette, often described as type V, includes broad shoulders and a pronounced bust with a narrow waist and slim hips and thighs. If you have this figure, your goal should be to highlight the lower body.

Not recommended:

- Blazers, blouses, and sweaters with padded shoulders
- Tops with thin straps
- Wide blouses, sweaters, and tunics
- Pencil skirts
- Pants with a very narrow cut

Recommended:

- Dark blouses with a V-neckline
- Wide belts emphasizing the waist
- Jackets and coats with a straight-cut
- Skirts and trousers with patterns (in light and bold colors)
- Outfits that show off the legs

Clothes for V-Silhouette

IV.
Eight Iconic Styles
of Classic Elegance

The wardrobe of women is characterized by an extraordinary diversity of styles and trends that are constantly evolving. Such a wide range of options makes it impossible to describe them all. Some styles overlap, combining various inspirations and influences, while others draw deeply from forms and patterns known from the history of fashion.

Moreover, many styles go through fashion cycles, sometimes remaining on the sidelines for several years, only to triumphantly return with new energy and popularity. Some of these trends may resurface years later, adapting to changing preferences and societal needs, while others may be completely forgotten, only to be rediscovered by subsequent generations.

It is precisely this dynamic nature of fashion that makes the world of women's clothing fascinating and constantly evolving. It gives women the opportunity to express their individuality through attire, allowing them to experiment with different styles and create their own unique images.

English heiress or safari lady? Dandy woman, airy and romantic, or Parisian? Lady on a yacht, star on the red carpet, or lover of ethnic climates? On the following pages, you will find presentations of selected styles of classic elegance that hold an honorable place in fashion history. These described clothing conventions deserve attention not only because of their timelessness but also because of the exceptional character they possess.

Style 1: English Heiress

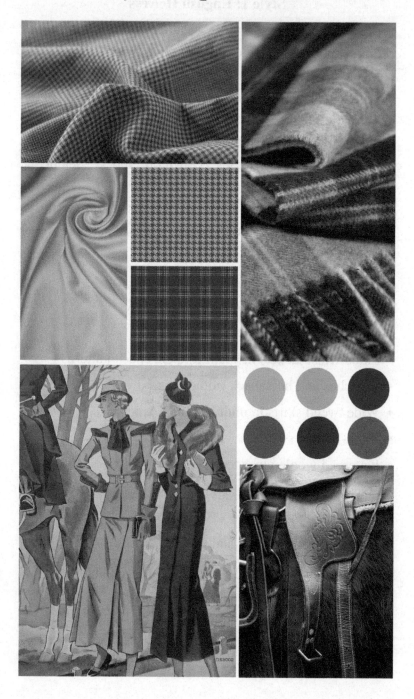

Style 1: English Heiress

A rustic atmosphere amidst beautiful nature. Horseback riding, long walks through the countryside, and close contact with nature. A lady dressed in this style, also known as English Country Style, evokes the atmosphere of an aristocratic estate away from the urban hustle and bustle. This ambiance can be found, among other places, in the British period drama series "Downton Abbey," set in the estate of Lord Grantham from 1912 to 1926. American designer Ralph Lauren showcased his fascination with the style of the British countryside in the autumn-winter 2012/2013 collection.

Characteristic elements of the style include:
- Clothing made of tweed and wool
- Fitted waist jackets in small English check patterns
- Breeches and horseback riding boots
- Wide tweed skirts in midi and maxi lengths
- Hand-knitted sweaters with distinctive textures
- Patterned woolen waistcoats
- Hats with narrow brims and berets
- Blouses with neckties
- Scarves with botanical and wildlife motifs
- Attire in earthy tones – shades of brown, beige, and green

Modern Interpretation of the Style 1

Style 1: English Heiress

What image does such a dressing style communicate?

- I enjoy life in rural seclusion – surrounded by nature.
- I like long walks, forest hikes, and horseback riding.
- I value natural fabrics that provide warmth and comfort.

Style 2: Safari Lady

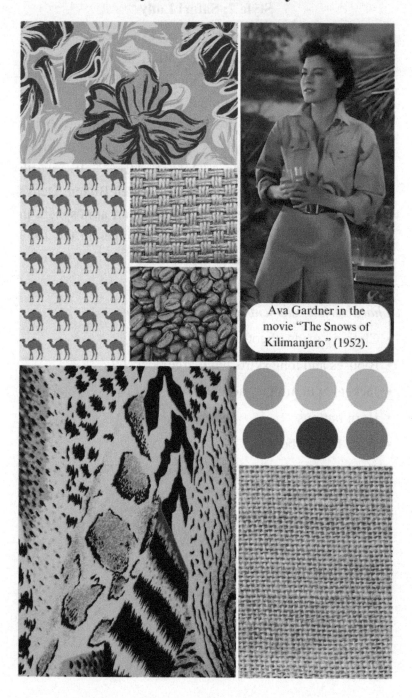

Ava Gardner in the movie "The Snows of Kilimanjaro" (1952).

Style 2: Safari Lady

African adventure, sun-drenched expanses, and wild animals. Comfort, protection against heat, and natural colors blending with the surroundings. This style, which harmonizes well with colonial architecture and interior design, was initiated by Europeans visiting overseas countries. The visual richness and atmosphere of that time are depicted in the film "Out of Africa." It's worth examining the attire of its characters: Karen Blixen, Denys Finch Hatton, and Berkeley Cole. The safari atmosphere in Kenya is also complemented by the costumes in the 1953 film "Mogambo" directed by John Ford.

Characteristic elements of the style include:
- Clothing made of cotton and linen
- Blouses and long skirts with large pockets
- Jackets with military accents
- Horn buttons
- Wide leather belts
- Crossbody bags resembling messenger bags
- Straw or cork hats
- Ankle-high hiking boots
- Attire in light natural colors – shades of off-white, sand, khaki, and faded brown

Modern Interpretation of the Style 2

Style 2: Safari Lady

What image does such a dressing style communicate?

- I enjoy comfortable clothing in natural colors.
- I love the sun, warmth, and tropical climates.
- I value natural and breathable fabrics.

Style 3: Dandy Woman

Marlene Dietrich in the movie
"Morocco" (1930).

Style 3: Dandy Woman

A wardrobe borrowed from the men's closet. Silhouettes and fabrics reminiscent of classic men's attire, enriched with a touch of feminine grace and playfulness. This style evokes the 19th century when male dandyism emerged. Refined dressing and elegant manners were promoted in that era by literary figures, including Charles Baudelaire, George Gordon Byron, Alfred de Musset, and Oscar Wilde. One of the dandies of the late 1950s is a character in the film "The Talented Mr. Ripley" – the impeccably dressed and life-enjoying Dick Greenleaf. The renowned fashion designer Coco Chanel and famous actresses like Marlene Dietrich and Katharine Hepburn also turned to clothing inspired by masculine elegance.

Characteristic elements of the style include:
- Clothing made of noble, heavier fabrics (twill, poplin)
- Suits and trouser sets
- Simple shirts: in white, light blue, or stripes
- Shoes such as loafers, brogues, oxfords, and derbies
- Ties, pocket squares, or scarves
- Hats in masculine styles (fedoras and panamas)
- Diplomat-style coats
- Subdued colors: graphite, brown, navy, black, and white.

Modern Interpretation of the Style 3

Style 3: Dandy Woman

What image does such a dressing style communicate?

- I am a confident, self-aware woman who knows her strengths.
- I appreciate good tailoring that highlights my assets.
- Silhouettes borrowed from men's wardrobes do not diminish my femininity.

Style 4: Airy and Romantic

Style 4: Airy and Romantic

Lightness, beautifully draping fabrics, floral patterns, and pastel or vibrant colors. The airy and romantic style has a long history. It was initiated by ladies draped in meters of fabric, clad in ancient Greek chitons and Roman tunics. Romanticism was highly valued by Rococo tailors. In the Empire era, women's fashion turned towards ancient traditions. The Biedermeier style brought abundant dresses with billowy sleeves made of airy fabrics. The Belle Époque era created ladies in romantic dresses and ornate hats. The Art Deco era introduced a fascination with tunics, reminiscent of ancient times. Romantic dresses with floral patterns appeared in fashion in the 1950s and 1970s.

Characteristic elements of the style include:
- Clothing made of flowing fabrics (muslin, chiffon, silk)
- Long and trailing dresses
- Floral patterns and other subtle designs
- Decorations such as bows, ties, and lace
- Billowy sleeves, ruching, and ruffles
- Romantic blouses with rounded collars
- Wide-brimmed hats
- Pastel colors (pink, peach, mint) or saturated hues (red, orange, purple)

Modern Interpretation of the Style 4

Style 4: Airy and Romantic

What image does such a dressing style communicate?

- I am proud to be a woman.
- I love outfits that suggest I have a romantic soul.
- I believe that femininity is the most important aspect of a woman's attire.

Style 5: Lady on a Yacht

Style 5: Lady on a Yacht

The whisper of wind and waves. The romantic perspective of a maritime adventure. This style solidified its position in fashion in the 1920s. Although the fascination with maritime adventures manifested itself in the second half of the 19th and early 20th centuries, evidenced by children's formal wear resembling sailor outfits in portraits from those times. However, the real revolution was initiated by the famous designer Coco Chanel, who in 1918 decided to bid farewell to restrictive clothing and began strolling along the seaside in Deauville in an outfit inspired by the attire of Normandy fishermen, consisting of a navy blue and white striped blouse and wide white trousers.

Characteristic elements of the style include:
- Clothing made of cotton, linen, poplin, and jersey
- Navy-blue and white striped blouses
- Chino, capri, or culottes pants
- Sweaters made of loosely woven cotton
- T-shirts with nautical motifs (stripes, anchors)
- Espadrilles, moccasins, or sneakers with white soles
- Small neckerchiefs, casually tied around the neck
- Straw hats with a flat crown and narrow brim
- Clothing in white, navy, red, and blue hues

Modern Interpretation of the Style 5

Style 5: Lady on a Yacht

What image does such a dressing style communicate?

- I love the atmosphere of seaside resorts and yacht harbors.
- I appreciate comfort, simple forms, and universal color combinations.
- I enjoy embracing classic clothing solutions.

Style 6: The Parisian Lady

Style 6: The Parisian Lady

Strolls along the chic sidewalks of the elegant city. Mornings with coffee and croissants, and evenings with exquisite dishes in beautiful restaurants. The style of the Parisian Lady is associated not only with great tailoring, famous designers, and spectacular fashion shows but also with everyday chic under the sign of noble comfort. Clothing in this convention represents a successful combination of excellent tailoring with comfort. They are based on classic solutions and modest elegance.

Characteristic elements of the style include:

- Clothing made of noble fabrics ensuring comfort (silk, wool, tweed, gabardine, cashmere, shantung, jacquard)
- Classic-cut shirt blouses
- A-line skirts knee-length or below-the-knee
- Pleated skirts
- Jacket-style blazers
- Cigarette pants
- Jewelry with pearls and colorless stones
- Flat or low-heeled shoes: pilgrim pumps, classic pumps, or ballerina flats (for more casual occasions)
- Clothing in white, beige, navy, graphite, ash, black, blue, red and blush pink

Modern Interpretation of the Style 6

Style 6: The Parisian Lady

What image does such a dressing style communicate?

- I appreciate classic elegance.
- In my attire, I want to feel chic and comfortable.
- I don't need to draw attention to myself to feel elegant.

Style 7: Red Carpet Star

Marylin Monroe

Style 7: Red Carpet Star

Elegant receptions, grand balls, premieres, and vernissages, solemn gatherings in the stylish company. Spectacular and lavish creations, long dresses, high-heeled shoes. The style of the red carpet star, also known as glamour, was born in the golden era of Hollywood. From the second half of the 1920s to the early 1960s, many films were made that are now considered classics. The elegance of that era was characterized by refined chic – without unnecessary flaunting of sexuality and dangerous balancing on the edge of good taste.

Characteristic elements of the style include:
- Clothing made of taffeta, satin, muslin, and chiffon
- Flowing silhouettes gently draping the figure
- Long dresses with bare shoulders or backs
- Ruching, ruffles, and puffs
- Ornaments such as scarves and bows
- Long shawls draped over the shoulders
- High-heeled shoes
- Statement jewelry (substantial necklaces, large earrings)
- Small clutch bags, pouches, or minaudieres
- Rich colors (navy, purple, dark green) or pastels (pink, blue, peach, mint, cream)

Modern Interpretation of the Style 7

Style 7: Red Carpet Star

What image does such a dressing style communicate?

- I have a special event or grand gala ahead.
- I emphasize the importance of the event with my festive attire.
- In clothing, I value elegance and meticulousness.

Style 8: Lover of Ethnic Vibes

Frida Kahlo

Style 8: Lover of Ethnic Vibes

Faraway travels to regions known not only for their beautiful landscapes but also for their meticulous approach to composing folk costumes. Dresses inspired by ethnic attire. Vivid and saturated colors, embroidery, ribbons, lace, and floral patterns. However, this style is not about transferring old models to modern clothing or choosing creations similar to those worn by folk groups, but about inspiration. Many fashion designers drew from folklore. One famous lover of ethnic vibes was Frida Kahlo. The painter referenced Mexican culture not only in her works but also in her attire. She adored colorful, pleated long dresses inspired by folk tradition.

Characteristic elements of the style include:
- Clothing made of cotton, linen, and lightweight wool
- Fabrics with patterns inspired by nature: flowers, leaves
- Saturated bold colors (red, yellow, orange, green, blue)
- Long dresses and skirts with ruffles
- Blouses with puffy sleeves
- Lace and colorful jacquard ribbons
- Wide belts accentuating the waist
- Jewelry made of colorful beads, wood, and shells

Modern Interpretation of the Style 8

Style 8: Lover of Ethnic Vibes

What image does such a dressing style communicate?

- I value tradition, so I gladly reach for outfits inspired by it.
- I enjoy freedom, nature, colors, and folk atmospheres.
- In clothing, I prefer unpretentiousness.

Mixing Conventions and Stylish Quotes

Eight of the most interesting fashion styles are described in this chapter. After acquainting with them, you're probably wondering which one to choose. The answer might be surprising: you don't have to decide on just one. You can select different conventions – depending on the occasion, situation, and mood.

While vacationing by the sea, you'll feel great in the style of a lady on a yacht – even if you don't spend a single day on board. During a weekend in the countryside, you can play the role of an English heiress, and at a garden party – in the convention of a lover of ethnic vibes. You'll accentuate the atmosphere of a summer vacation by embodying a lady on safari. At a professional meeting, you'll fit into the Parisian or feminine dandy convention. You'll brighten up an afternoon meeting with flowing and romantic attire and emphasize the festivity of an evening grand gala with a red-carpet star's outfit.

Also worth considering is the use of subtle quotes from different styles. A white-navy striped t-shirt, a scarf with a motif of wild birds, jewelry made of wooden beads, a straw hat, pilgrim pump shoes, a masculine-style watch, a wide-brimmed hat, or a box-shaped handbag can not only add character to a neutral outfit but also highlight your fondness for a particular clothing convention. If you want to emphasize that you value and like a specific style, you don't necessarily have to embody it from head to toe. A distinctive clothing element can say a lot – especially if it is accompanied by a neutral background (for example, a plain dress with a simple cut, a light-colored blouse, dark cigarette pants, or a classic jacket in a muted color).

However, it's worth warning any lady inclined to experiment not to indulge in fantasy too much. Combining multiple styles in a single outfit can lead to a chaotic mix that lacks elegance. When resorting to quotes, remember that they should represent only one style in a given clothing composition. A wide tweed skirt in the style of an English heiress doesn't go well with a sporty t-shirt, sneakers, ethnic shell bracelets, and a paisley scarf. In this case, we have a mixture of several styles. A strange composition is created by a chunky wool sweater with a tulle skirt, a pearl necklace, and hiking boots. In the described example, in addition to mixing styles, there is a disturbance in the balance of elements. The thick knit of the sweater and the sturdy shape of the shoes, along with the lightweight fabric of the skirt and formal jewelry, create an unfavorable contrast.

Keen trend observers will notice that contemporary fashion often resorts to solutions close to those described above. Stylists also excel in such compositions, breaking all the rules to emphasize their originality. Although such mixtures no longer surprise anyone today (they would have caused at least surprise forty-fifty years ago), it's worth keeping in mind that they don't fit into the canons of classicism. They may therefore be an expression of personal fantasy and a casual approach to rules, but – it must be emphasized – they will never be elegant.

Having Style vs Being Stylish

How can one balance incorporating different styles and subtly referencing various conventions while maintaining elegance and fashion? In answering this question, it's worth examining "having style" and "being stylish." Although both phrases can be treated as synonyms, there is a subtle difference between them. The concept of "having style" suggests that a person has developed (after years of trial and error) a certain wardrobe convention characteristic to them, in which they present themselves to the surroundings. The phrase "being stylish" means that by defining oneself as such, a lady chooses attention-grabbing outfits that distinguish her from other women, who opt for conventional clothing solutions.

However, possessing one's style or being stylish is not synonymous with having a sense of elegance, nor does it defend against fashion blunders. Not every approach to conventions and trends is synonymous with good taste. Sometimes, we too easily succumb to what is fashionable, popular, and offered in clothing stores without considering whether a particular style suits us and emphasizes good taste. One can derive joy from fashion provided it is approached sensibly. It's not worth becoming a slave to trends. Not everything it offers should be accepted because not every proposal is tasteful. One should not approach it rigidly because a lack of flexibility can backfire. From every trend and style, it's worth drawing what is best and most interesting for oneself.

Five Stylish Tips

How can you approach fashion and trends to find joy in creating outfits? Here are five tips to remember while developing your style.

Tip 1

Embrace fashion wholeheartedly, but maintain a sense of moderation in your approach. Treat novelties with skepticism.

Tip 2

Explore the possibilities offered by different clothing styles. Remember, you don't have to settle for just one.

Tip 3

Tailor your clothing style to the situation you find yourself in. Also, adapt it to your mood.

Tip 4

Approach fashion with freedom and flexibility. Be cautious not to become a thoughtless imitator of it.

Tip 5

Remember to have fun with fashion and the trends it offers. Such an approach will bring you much joy in styling.

V.

The Palette of Elegance:
Crafting Stylish Combinations

The Power of Associations and Emotional Play

Colors play a crucial role in fashion style, as they have the extraordinary power to evoke feelings and elicit connotations. Although from a physiological standpoint, they are merely perceived by the eye as electromagnetic radiation within the visible light spectrum, it is impossible to deny their impact on the soul and emotional state. Hence, it is not surprising that the theory of color is a discipline that encompasses not only physics and biology but also psychology.

Colors evoke strong associations – both positive and negative – deeply rooted in culture and capable of playing on emotions. The expressive red is not only the color of love and passion but also war and revolution. It attracts attention, yet an excess of it can be irritating. Classic black is associated with both elegance and formality, as well as mourning and dirt. It can build an elegant and somber image. Pure white is the color of innocence and purity, yet it is also cold and reminiscent of snow. It captivates with its sterility, yet it gives the impression of coldness. Warm and expressive yellow and orange are the colors of high temperatures and optimism, yet they can be overwhelming in their expressiveness. Green is associated with nature. The family of blue and gray hues creates an impression of sobriety and competence in attire, yet it often faces criticism for being cold and distant. Pink and purple are synonymous with charm and femininity, yet in excess, they can create an overly sweet image. Safe brown can be perceived as too mundane and sad. Colors often evoke extreme associations and emotions.

Temperature, Shades, and Illusions

The classification of colors is served by the commonly used Natural Color System (NCS), developed by Ewald Hering. The German physiologist created a wheel of four primary colors: red, yellow, green, and blue. When mixed, they build an extensive palette of colors. The wheel does not include white and black because they are formed by combining the primary colors.

The line crossing the wheel delineates the boundary between warm colors (yellow, orange, red) and cool colors (green, blue, purple). The first category comprises hues from the red and yellow palette, while the second includes shades from the green and blue families.

However, color classification relies not only on their temperature (warm-cool) but also on their shade (light – containing a large amount of white, and dark – containing more black) and saturation (saturated – rich in pigment, and muted – with a grayish hue). Colors are also described

Color Wheel

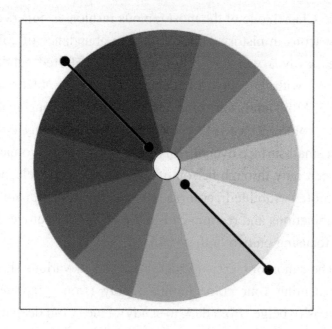

using other terms. Juicy shades are vivid and intense. Pastel colors are diluted and subtle. Neon colors can be strikingly vibrant. Dirty colors, on the other hand, have a tint of brown, gray, or black.

Colors evoke optical illusions concerning movement, contrast, and weight. Warm colors (yellow, orange, and red) appear to advance, unlike cool colors (blue and green), which recede into the background. Shades with the same saturation seem more or less pronounced depending on their surroundings. Objects in shades of blue and green appear lighter than elements in red tones.

Base Palette of Classic Elegance

Coco Chanel, one of the most famous fashion designers and style icons in history, believed that an abundance of colors takes away a woman's originality. She preferred subdued colors, with her favorite combination being black and white. Although fashion and aesthetics have nothing against using colors, it is worth considering that too many colors on a small surface overwhelms and can cause the woman to be seen only through her outfit. Therefore, classic elegance promotes subdued colors. It favors monochromatic combinations and recommends not mixing too many colors but focusing on two or three at most.

The canon of classic elegance consists of various shades representing four color families: gray (from graphite to light ash), beige (from dark to sandy), blue (from deep navy to sky blue), and brown (from rich chocolate to faded cocoa). Also included are white and black along with all their variations. These are colors that have remained fashionable for decades.

Colors belonging to the canon of classics are subdued, or dirty, as well as muted. It is precisely in their calm character that the essence of elegance lies, which by definition should not be imposing. A lady in a subdued dress in noble navy blue, surrounded by accessories in beige, always looks much more elegant than a woman in a vivid red or eye-catching green outfit.

Base Palette
of Classic Elegance

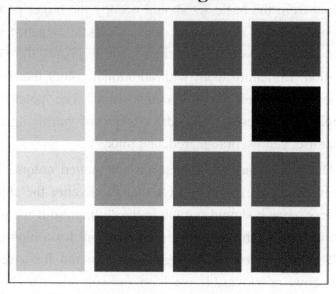

SupplementaryPalette
of Classic Elegance

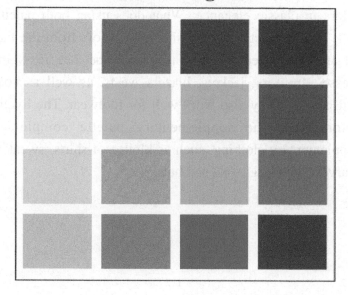

Supplementary Palette of Elegance

Colors from the basic set should occupy the larger part of the outfit – this is what the rules of classic elegance say. You can limit yourself to them, but it is not the only solution. Enriching them with additional colors that bring variety and liven up the composition. The palette of supplementary colors includes shades of purple, green, turquoise, yellow, orange, red, and pink.

This set includes both intense and muted colors. The canon of classic elegance says that the livelier the shade, the less space it should occupy in the styling. So if we want to complement the outfit with red, let's opt for a blouse in a darker wine color, keeping the vibrant red for a scarf, belt, bow, or gloves. If we long for yellow, let's choose a dress in a straw or mustard shade, reserving canary yellow for a scarf, bracelet, or bag.

Let's return to the basic and supplementary palette of colors in classic elegance. What does using both palettes look like in practice? Well, the calm colors from the base set are best suited for the basic wardrobe, i.e., for skirts, dresses, trousers, jackets, blazers, vests, as well as coats and jackets. They also work well for footwear. The livelier colors from the supplementary palette complement supplementary clothing, such as blouses, t-shirts, sweaters, scarves, shawls, gloves, and hats.

Colors and the Code of Classic Elegance

Looking at the subdued base palette of elegant colors, one might wonder whether a lady should wear garments in intense, eye-catching colors. Of course, she should. The choice of clothing colors depends on the situation: professional work and business relationships require different colors from us, while we can afford others in casual and outdoor settings.

Although subdued shades from the base palette are considered the colors of elegance, nothing is stopping us from reaching for more standout clothing in certain situations. Such occasions include formal receptions, picnics, outdoor gatherings, dinners in restaurant gardens, and cheerful events organized in spring and summer (weddings, baptisms, parties, and children's birthdays).

The more formal the situation, the more subdued the clothing colors should be. Therefore, it is worth reaching for subdued shades of blue, gray, beige, and brown during business meetings, professional conferences, and job interviews, as well as cocktails, banquets, formal dinners, and evening parties.

However, there is a certain category of colors with an exceptionally inelegant character. These are neon colors, associated with reflective vests worn by service personnel: sharp yellow, eye-catching bright green, intense orange, and vivid pink. A wardrobe in such assertive shades contradicts the canon of classic elegance.

The Art of Color Composition

Skillful color composition is an essential element of elegance. It's easy to see that the right combinations add sophistication and bring out class. While ill-conceived or tasteless ones can overshadow the beauty of even the most chic wardrobe pieces. Therefore, it's worth taking a closer look at the ways of composing colors. All methods are universal, not limited to clothing but also applicable to interior design, decorations, and artistic creation.

There are several techniques for combining colors. Colors can be paired in a complementary or harmonious way. In both cases, knowledge of their arrangement on the color wheel is helpful. They can also be composed monochromatically, using various shades from the same family. Also noteworthy are combinations with strong contrast and the pairing of basic colors with accentuating ones. Below are descriptions of each of the five mentioned techniques along with examples.

Method 1: Complementary.

This method involves combining colors found on opposite sides of the wheel. Complementary compositions include: yellow with purple, orange with blue, and red with green. Pairing colors from opposite sides of the wheel also involves compiling shades of different temperatures (for example, hot orange with cold blue).

Example: Green with red.

Although this color combination is not commonly considered classic, it still makes a good composition. Green and red are so-called complementary colors. They are located on opposite sides of the color wheel. Despite being a strong and bold contrast to each other, they still create a successful whole.

Method 2: Monochromatism.

Following this technique involves choosing colors from the same family. Monochromatic combinations consist of different shades of the same color. Such compilations include blue with navy, light pink with fuchsia, cream with yellow, and light purple with dark plum. Monochromatic combinations also include more colors from one family (for example, several shades of blue).

Example: Monochromatic combinations in clothing.

Outfits from head to toe in one color are elegant, even sophisticated. However, if a monochromatic outfit lacks diversity, we can opt for fabrics with different textures (for example, pair smooth pants with a sweater with a pronounced weave in the same color) and accessories (enrich the outfit with bold jewelry).

Method 3: Harmony.

This method involves combining colors next to each other on the wheel. Harmonious compositions include yellow with orange, yellow with green, and blue with purple. Because adjacent colors share many similarities, such compilations are a safe choice.

Example: Breaking conventions.

An excellent way to create non-obvious color combinations is through art, which teaches us that unconventional compositions can work. By opening up to painting – not only from centuries past but also contemporary – we can see how boldly artists approach this matter. They possess an extraordinary sense of color, from intuition, knowledge, and excellent preparation.

Method 4: Contrast.

This type of composition is based on two colors characterized by distinct opposites. One color is dark and intense, while the other is light and delicate. The most famous contrasting combination is black and white. Less popular but beautiful combinations include white with graphite, ecru with navy, and beige with black.

Example: Stylish contrasts.

White with black, ash with navy, and beige with brown are popular combinations. Each of the two colors in a contrasting combination plays its role: the dark one adds sophistication, while the light one adds brightness. When thinking about the role of colors with more white, remember that garments in these shades work well near the face – as a collar, blouse, or scarf.

Method 5: Base plus accent.

This style involves choosing a leading color that plays the main role and enriching it with a modest addition of another color. The base can be one of the quiet colors of classicism (navy, brown, graphite), while the accent can be a lively and vibrant shade, which in the canon of elegance occupies one of the last places (including orange, yellow, light green).

Example: French composition.

The combination of white, blue, and red is called French – because it appears on the flag of this country. This classic combination of complementary colors, synonymous with elegance, fits perfectly into chic creations with a touch of fantasy. Blue and red, found on the flag of France, are the traditional colors of Paris, while white symbolizes royal power.

Color Combinations and Time of Day and Environment

Certain color compositions are suitable for specific times of the day. The rules of classic elegance suggest that colors should change as the hours pass. Bright colors work well in the mornings and early afternoons, while darker colors suit afternoons and evenings better. During a carnival ball, a dress in dark wine, rich navy, bottle green, or classic black looks much better than a creation in white, sandy beige, or ecru. During a mid-morning social meeting in a café, a blouse in a pastel color looks favorable. In such a situation a dark-colored outfit may seem too formal or gloomy.

A similar rule applies to outdoor gatherings and events organized indoors. For a summer afternoon garden party, it's better to choose an outfit in bright and vibrant colors. Dark and muted colors are preferred when planning meetings in dimly lit and discreetly illuminated interiors. Such colors look beautiful in the glow of subtle lamps and candles on tables.

Bright and Dark Colors and Elegance

The most elegant combinations include colors representing extreme saturations: very light and dark. Equally chic are compositions composed solely of pale or highly saturated colors.

Examples of the first category include commonly liked compositions: white with black, white with navy, beige with black, beige with navy, ecru with graphite, ecru with black. The dark color plays a foundational role in them, creating an impression of sophistication and seriousness. The light color adds freshness and a touch of lightness to the combination. Classic examples of such color compositions include outfits signaling the uniqueness of the situation: a white blouse with a navy skirt (as a formal schoolgirl outfit) and a black suit with a white shirt (as a festive attire).

Examples of the second category are monochromatic compositions, such as white with ecru, ecru with beige, white with beige, navy with black, and graphite with black. Styling in the lightest colors from the palette creates an image of freshness and sterility. It also suggests that the attire is maintained in perfect cleanliness (after all, even the smallest stain is visible on fabrics in such colors), and the person wearing it is meticulous. A woman in a white dress or cream coat always attracts attention. Styling in the darkest colors emphasizes seriousness and formality. A lady dressed from head to toe in black with a touch of graphite or navy stands out against the backdrop of brightly dressed individuals.

Attention-Grabbing Compositions

Certain colors are so intense in expression that they cannot go unnoticed. Therefore, if you intend to draw attention to yourself or a specific detail of an outfit (for example, a particular garment), opt for specific compositions.

Vivid and bright colors stand out against muted and dark hues. This rule applies to red when paired with black, navy, graphite, and brown radiates strength and captures attention. This principle is utilized by individuals speaking at business conferences and other public forums. A red tie on a politician or a scarf with a red pattern on a speaker has the remarkable power to draw the audience's gaze. Interestingly, garments in this color attract attention to the facial area, which is crucial for public speakers and performers. Similar, albeit significantly milder effects, are observed with saturated orange, vibrant yellow, and intense fuchsia.

Many examples of this color trick can be found in politics. Not only do the red ties of politicians serve as focal points during debates, but also multicolored and shiny brooches (which were famously worn by the former British Prime Minister Margaret Thatcher).

About a Certain Color Trick

The most important role is the color closest to the face. It influences the perception of the entire outfit and determines whether we look good or not. Therefore, it's not just the shades of blouses, sweaters, and jackets that matter, but also scarves, hats, and hair bands. The colors of jewelry items closest to the face, such as earrings, clips, necklaces, and brooches, also play a crucial role.

Knowing this rule, you can employ a color trick when composing your wardrobe. For example, if you know that black doesn't suit you well, but the situation calls for an outfit in that color, opt for a scarf around your neck in a color that complements your complexion better. You can also go for a string of pearls (which always brightens) or a shiny brooch. If your silhouette looks good in dark skirts and pants but dark shades don't suit you well, ensure the top part of your outfit is in one of the colors that harmonize well with your complexion. Remember that a light element close to the face adds brightness and freshness, while a vibrant one adds energy and expression.

Colors and Combinations

Let's take a closer look at individual colors. Due to the multitude of shades, the characteristics of each can be seen as an attempt to encompass the entire color family.

Red

Red is the most expressive color in the palette, associated with strong emotions and feelings: love, passion, and ardor.

Clothing items in this color attract attention even in small doses. In large amounts, they can be tiring to the eye and even cause unease. Red effectively enlivens and radiates an aura of energy around the wearer. It softens with noble colors such as navy, graphite, and ash, creating elegant combinations.

Red creates classic combinations with white, black, blue, and gray. It interestingly complements beige, brown, green, and turquoise. In classic attire, red serves as a strong statement accessory or eye-catching accent and a clothing element that plays a supporting role (otherwise, it creates too imposing an image).

Red looks great on women with jet-black hair. It also suits blondes with a tanned complexion. Blondes with a pinkish complexion or redheads should avoid it.

Yellow

Yellow is associated with the sun, pleasant air temperature, and fresh fruits (lemons, bananas, and pears). It warms up the image, adds energy, and creates an impression of optimism. Marketing experts call it the color of communication because it fosters openness and encourages dialogue. Even a small clothing item in this color (scarf, hat, cap) brightens the attire, cheers up on a cloudy day, and reminds of summer.

Yellow creates classic compositions with blue, navy, orange, brown, and green. Unconventional combinations are formed with white, purple, gray, burgundy, and black.

In clothing, yellow serves as an eye-catching and invigorating accent. This color complements clothing with a holiday vibe perfectly. It goes well with a tan.

Warm, honey shades of yellow add sophistication to brunettes with an olive complexion. Cool tones, with a hint of green, highlight the beauty of blonde hair.

Green

Although green is one of the most popular clothing colors, it's challenging to match with most skin tones. When choosing clothing in this color, it's important to note that it may not always look good near the face – for example as a scarf, collar, or headgear (it may accentuate pallor and emphasize skin imperfections). Green has a wide range of shades: from sage to lime, mint, malachite, olive, to emerald.

This color forms classic combinations with yellow, orange, purple, navy, and black. It creates interesting compositions with beige, pink, red, burgundy, and gray.

Green serves as an eye-catching and invigorating accent in clothing. Its darker shades are suitable for evening wear. Green is the perfect color for outdoor holiday clothing.

Redheads and blondes with a golden hue look great in green. It also suits green- and blue-eyed brunettes.

Blue

All shades of blue have a cooling effect. They cool down the temperature of neighboring warm colors (for example, orange). They reveal true elegance when combined with so-called broken colors (which include creamy, sandy, and maroon).

Blue forms classic compositions with white, navy, red, yellow, pink, and black. Paired with beige, orange, green, gray, or brown, it creates unconventional and beautiful compositions.

Blue is a classic clothing color that inspires trust and enhances competence. As an accessory, it invigorates attire. It works wonderfully in outdoor holiday clothing.

Blue accentuates the beauty of blue-eyed blondes. It also looks good on brunettes and redheads.

Orange

Orange is a color that stimulates appetite. It is associated with juicy and sweet fruits: oranges, tangerines, peaches, apricots, papayas, and persimmons. It also refers to healthy vegetables: carrots, pumpkins, and bell peppers. Its influence on the sense of taste is appreciated by creators of food product packaging (such as juices, purees, and sweets) and interior decorators designing dining areas, bars, and restaurants.

This vibrant color forms classic combinations with navy, blue, burgundy, brown, and yellow. It creates interesting compositions with gray, purple, beige, turquoise, green, and black.

Orange in clothing attracts attention, brightens up, and brightens the outfit. It works well in holiday clothing.

Orange looks best on dark-eyed brunettes. Dark blondes with an olive complexion can also opt for it.

Purple

Purple has many shades: from dark purple to deep red. For centuries, it has been associated with power and wealth – partly because obtaining its dye was laborious and costly. Purple robes were worn by emperors, kings, and church dignitaries. The motif of a fairy or witch wearing a dress of this color often appears in fairy tales. Purple adds dignity and mystery to the image.

With navy, black, blue, gray, and white, it forms classic combinations. It creates interesting compositions with beige, yellow, orange, green, brown, and burgundy.

Purple serves as an accessory or eye-catching accent in everyday clothing. In evening wear, it emphasizes the specialness of the occasion.

Purple beautifully highlights the beauty of redheaded women. It also suits brunettes with an olive complexion.

Navy blue

Navy blue is called the color of diplomacy. This is because it is often chosen in the world of politics. Meetings of representatives at the highest levels (national and international) show that navy is the most common color for suits. This color is also loved in the business world – especially in banking and finance.

Navy creates classic combinations of white, blue, red, pink, yellow, and orange. It's also worth combining with beige, green, turquoise, purple, gray, and brown.

Navy blue serves as a basic clothing color. It emphasizes the seriousness of the situation. Navy clothing inspires trust and indicates professional competence.

The most universal shade that suits all types of beauty is light navy blue.

Pink

Pink is the color most associated with women and femininity, delicacy, and sweetness. It has a wide range of shades: from subtle powdery to intense fuchsia. The more saturated the better it highlights distinct beauty. The lighter it is, the more it enhances the beauty of delicate types. In the case of pink clothing, much depends on the cut and fabric. A formal dress in a classic cut made of solid fabric (such as wool, gabardine, silk, and shantung) does not deserve to be childish.

Pink creates classic compositions with white, black, blue, navy, purple, and gray. Unconventional compositions are formed with beige, yellow, orange, green, brown, and burgundy.

This color attracts attention, enlivens every outfit, and highlights the lightness of the creation or the freedom of the situation. It works well as a clothing color for spring and summer.

Blondes with a pinkish complexion should avoid clothing in this color. Redheads also don't look favorable in it.

Brown

Contrary to appearances, brown is not one of the so-called easy colors. Although it works perfectly in interior design, creating a restrained but conservative image, it can give the impression of overwhelm by clothing. The reason is its stability. Since brown does not go well with every type of beauty, it should be used carefully. Interestingly, it's also used sparingly in men's clothing: you won't find it, for example, in the world of politics and business, nor is it suitable for solemn occasions and high-ranking events.

Brown forms classic compositions with beige, yellow, orange, green, and burgundy. It creates interesting compositions with pink, purple, navy, gray, red, blue, and white.

Brown serves as a basic element of clothing. It emphasizes the seriousness of the situation. Clothing in brown indicates stability.

When choosing clothing in this color, it's worth looking at its shade. Warm, honey shades complement ladies with hair in a similar tone. Cool variations go well with the beauty of women with hair in a similar hue.

Beige

Beige is one of the most elegant colors. It is subdued, subtle, and has a non-imposing character. It warms up the complexion and softens facial features. It adds elegance and gentleness to the image. As a clothing color, it looks good in casual and formal situations. Although it does not belong to the group of classic business colors (which include primarily navy, graphite, ash, and blue), it still finds its place in professional situations. A women's suit, blazer, or dress in beige creates a professional image.

Beige pairs well with brown, white, black, burgundy, red, navy, and green. It creates interesting combinations with pink, purple, gray, blue, orange, and yellow.

Beige serves as a basic element of clothing. It builds an image of calm elegance and adds lightness to outfits.

This color suits blondes, brunettes, redheads, and dark-haired women. However, if its shade resembles hair color, it's worth breaking up such a monochromatic composition with a bold accessory.

Gray

Gray stands in many ways in opposition to brown. It finds wide application both in modern interiors and in clothing. Dark shades of this elegant color appear in politics, diplomacy, and business, as well as during solemn occasions and high-ranking events. Gray symbolizes restraint, control of emotions, and dignity. Since an excess of it can be overwhelming, it's recommended to combine it with other, more vibrant colors.

Gray is a very versatile color. It pairs well with almost all colors. Traditionally, it is paired with black, white, red, pink, and purple. It is presented interestingly with yellow, orange, burgundy, beige, brown, green, and blue.

Gray serves as a basic component of clothing. It is a color that emphasizes seriousness and professional competence. Its addition can calm down the color of an outfit.

Light blondes and women with red and jet-black hair look best in gray. Women with less distinct hair color should break up the gray clothing with a bold-colored accessory.

White

White, symbolizing purity and innocence in common understanding, undoubtedly adds freshness. A creation in this color looks neat, suggests precision, and emphasizes the festivity of the occasion. Contrary to appearances, white is not boring, because in addition to the classic, pure variety, it has many shades of so-called broken colors, enriched with the glow of another color. They can have not only a cold but also a warm character. For example, the shade of ivory has a warming effect because it contains a drop of yellow. The platinum variation includes a hint of gray, making it cool. An intermediate shade is ecru, which has yellow and gray reflections. Interestingly, this is the color of unbleached silk, and its name comes from the French word "écru," meaning raw canvas.

White creates classic compositions with black, navy, red, blue, pink, purple, and gray. It forms interesting combinations with beige, yellow, orange, brown, burgundy, and green.

Classic Color Combinations

White brightens up dark elements of the outfit. It emphasizes the lightness of the creation. It works well as a clothing color for the day.

Although this color goes well with every hair color, it emphasizes pallor. It looks great on blondes with an olive or tanned complexion. Creamy and ivory shades add radiance to the face.

Black

Black is a color full of contradictions. On the one hand, it is traditionally the color of mourning in our cultural circle; on the other hand, it is considered the most elegant color (especially during ceremonies and high-ranking events). Black is beloved by fashion designers and creators of various kinds: notice that many designers appear in public wearing it. Some connoisseurs believe it is the perfect color to hide behind. The fact is that black does not impose itself and is a background color. Like white, it has shades. The darkest variation is classic black. A lower saturation level is ebony, which contains a drop of brown. English soot is the darkest shade of matte black, while smoky is the darkest shade of glossy black.

Black works well in classic combinations with white, red, blue, pink, gray, purple, and green. It presents uniquely with yellow, orange, navy, and beige.

Black serves as the base color of styling and in accessories. Since it highlights the uniqueness of the situation, it is suitable as a clothing color for the evening.

Blondes with fair complexions look great in this color. Brunettes and brunettes who opt for black clothing should complement it with a bold accessory or shiny jewelry.

Color Analysis – Does It Make Sense?

In recent years, the assessment of individual natural beauty colors has made a stunning career in selecting clothing and makeup colors. Color analysis, limited to four seasons, has expanded to twelve types. Attributes related to temperature, value, and chromaticity have been assigned to them. In this way, two light types (light spring and light summer), two warm types (warm spring and warm autumn), two pure types (pure spring and pure winter), two cool types (cool summer and cool winter), two deep types (deep autumn and deep winter), and two muted types (muted summer and muted autumn) were created.

The variety of these types causes many people to become lost in their maze. Color analysis has as many advocates as opponents. The former passionately creates color palettes corresponding to each of the twelve types. The latter, however, criticize this analysis for its high level of complexity, which requires hiring a specialist to understand one's style. They suggest focusing on colors we feel best when choosing wardrobe colors. They also recommend paying attention primarily to the temperature of colors because certain types of beauty look better in warm colors, while others look better in cool ones.

The method of choosing clothing and makeup colors is therefore usually the result of personal choice. Of course, you can undergo individual color analysis performed by a professional. However, no assurance opting for colors within their prescribed palette will result in an elegant look. After all, color is just one of many elements of elegance, and not all shades fit into its classic canons. You can also follow an individual path based on your preferences and experiences. Such a behavior also does not guarantee elegance, but it does not exclude it either.

Clothing Color and Skin Tone

Clothing colors can be chosen to match hair and eye color. However, one should not forget the skin tone, which plays an equally important role. Therefore, it is worth examining its natural shade – without makeup.

Healthy, slightly rosy, or tanned skin blends well with cool colors, which enhance its tone through contrast. Warm colors complement its natural hue perfectly. These skin tones mix well with white, black, gray, beige, and brown. Delicate, light skin does not pair well with bright colors, as they emphasize its paleness. Soft and muted colors work well with this complexion. Light colors in warm shades also look good. If the skin has a yellowish or reddish hue, it is necessary to choose clothing colors very carefully. Cool variations bring out unfavorable nuances. Red looks bad. It's better to opt for non-contrasting colors. Black and white don't look good right next to the face.

VI.

Iconic Women of Elegance:
Profiles of Twenty Stylish Figures

Coco Chanel

Coco Chanel revolutionized the fashion world in the 20th century, becoming one of the most influential figures in fashion history. Her style, combining simplicity with elegance, remains timeless and inspires fashion enthusiasts.

Early Years and Revolutionary Style

Coco Chanel began her career as a hat designer, opening her first shop in Paris in 1910. Her early designs were simpler and more functional than the fashion of the time, immediately attracting women seeking comfort and elegance. Chanel introduced simplicity to fashion, a true revolution in an era when women wore complicated, uncomfortable outfits. Her designs, such as simple jersey dresses, became synonymous with modern elegance.

Evolution of Style

Coco Chanel's style evolved but always maintained simplicity and elegance. Chanel was a pioneer in creating unisex fashion, incorporating elements of men's wardrobes into women's fashion, such as blazers, trousers, and shirts. Her famous tweed suits, with clean lines and precise tailoring, symbolized class and sophistication. Chanel also introduced the little black dress, a staple in women's wardrobes, symbolizing elegance and versatility.

Casual and Charisma

Coco Chanel was also known for her casual style, which combined elegance with comfort. Often seen in simple yet stylish outfits such as jersey blazers, straightforward skirts, and white shirts, Chanel demonstrated that fashion could be practical and beautiful. Her lifestyle inspired many women who wanted to look elegant without sacrificing comfort.

Stylish Fashion Ambassador

Chanel not only revolutionized fashion with her designs but also became an ambassador for a new approach to fashion and life. Her philosophy that "fashion fades, only style remains" became a mantra for many in the fashion industry. Coco Chanel was also known for her unique approach to accessories, introducing costume jewelry that was elegant yet accessible. Her famous pearls, gold chains, and iconic double "C" logo became fashion symbols.

Legacy of Style

The legacy of Coco Chanel is immense and enduring. Her fashion house, founded over a century ago, remains one of the most important and influential in the fashion world, under the leadership of outstanding designers such as Karl Lagerfeld and Virginie Viard. Chanel No. 5, introduced in 1921, remains one of the most famous and best-selling perfumes in the world. Her influence on fashion is evident in every collection celebrating simplicity, elegance, and functionality.

Louise Brooks

Louise Brooks, the iconic actress of the 1920s, is renowned for her distinctive style that epitomized the flapper era. Her unique blend of modernity, sophistication, and boldness continues to inspire fashion enthusiasts and designers.

Early Years and Emergence of Signature Style

Louise Brooks began her career as a dancer before transitioning to acting, gaining prominence in the silent film era. Her early style was characterized by the quintessential flapper look, which was revolutionary. She was known for her sleek, bobbed haircut, which became her signature and a defining feature of 1920s fashion. Her androgynous yet feminine style, featuring drop-waist dresses, cloche hats, and Mary Jane shoes, solidified her status as a trendsetter.

Evolution of Style

As her career progressed, Brooks' style evolved while maintaining its core elements of modernity and elegance. She often wore simple, streamlined dresses that highlighted her slim figure and complemented her bold haircut. Her wardrobe choices reflected the liberated spirit of the 1920s, embracing both femininity and a certain boyish charm. Louise favored monochrome outfits, geometric patterns, and luxurious fabrics like silk and satin, which added a touch of sophistication to her avant-garde style. Her impact on fashion extended beyond her film roles, influencing everyday women's fashion.

Casual and Charisma

Even in casual settings, Louise Brooks exuded an effortless chicness that captivated audiences. Her off-screen attire often included comfortable yet stylish pieces like loose trousers, blouses, and knitwear, which were unconventional for women in that period. Her relaxed yet fashionable approach to casual wear resonated with the youth of the era, who admired her for breaking traditional fashion norms. Brooks' charisma was evident in her sartorial choices, reinforcing her image as a modern woman.

Stylish Ambassador of the Jazz Age

Louise Brooks was a quintessential ambassador of the Jazz Age, embodying the cultural and social changes of the 1920s through her style. Her fashion choices reflected the decade's spirit of liberation and defiance against societal norms. Her style was not just about clothing but also about attitude, representing the newfound freedom and vibrancy of the post-war generation. She played a significant role in popularizing the flapper style globally.

Legacy of Style

The legacy of Louise Brooks as a style icon is enduring and profound. Her distinctive look and choices influence contemporary fashion, with designers and stylists frequently drawing inspiration from her iconic bob and flapper dresses. Brooks' ability to encapsulate the essence of the 1920s through her fashion has ensured her lasting relevance and admiration.

Elsa Schiaparelli

Elsa Schiaparelli, the legendary Italian fashion designer, remains one of the most influential style icons of the 20th century. Her avant-garde designs and fearless approach to fashion revolutionized the industry.

Early Years and Artistic Beginnings

Elsa Schiaparelli entered the fashion world in the 1920s. Influenced by the Surrealist movement, her early work was characterized by bold, unconventional designs that challenged traditional fashion norms. Schiaparelli's collaborations with artists like Salvador Dalí and Jean Cocteau resulted in some of her most iconic pieces, such as the Lobster Dress and the Tear Dress. Her early years were defined by a desire to blend art and fashion, creating wearable works of art that pushed boundaries.

Evolution of Style

Elsa Schiaparelli's style evolved, but her commitment to innovation and creativity remained constant. She introduced several groundbreaking concepts to fashion, including synthetic materials, bold color palettes, and whimsical motifs. Schiaparelli's designs often featured unexpected elements, such as the famous "shoe hat," which was a hat shaped like a high-heeled shoe. She was also known for her pioneering use of zippers as a fashion statement rather than just a functional element. Her collections were characterized by their daring silhouettes, intricate detailing, and a sense of humor.

Casual and Charisma

Elsa Schiaparelli was also known for her style, which was as bold and distinctive as her designs. Her off-duty looks often included tailored suits, statement accessories, and bold colors. Schiaparelli had a penchant for dramatic jewelry, commonly wearing oversized pieces that reflected her love for art and design. Her casual style was an extension of her creative spirit, blending elegance with a touch of eccentricity.

Stylish Innovator and Visionary

Elsa Schiaparelli was a visionary who saw fashion as an art form and used her designs to challenge conventions. She introduced the concept of themed collections, creating cohesive, story-driven designs that captivated audiences and set new standards in fashion. Schiaparelli's bold use of color, particularly her signature "shocking pink," became synonymous with her brand and a symbol of her daring creativity.

Legacy of Style

The legacy of Elsa Schiaparelli as a style icon is enduring and immensely influential. Her avant-garde designs and fearless approach to fashion continue to inspire modern designers and fashion lovers. Numerous exhibitions, books, and retrospectives have been dedicated to her life and work, highlighting her lasting impact on the fashion world. Schiaparelli's ability to blend art and fashion, along with her commitment to innovation, has left an indelible mark on the industry.

Marlene Dietrich

Marlene Dietrich, the legendary German-American actress and singer, remains one of the most enduring style icons of the 20th century. Her androgynous elegance continues to inspire designers and fashion enthusiasts worldwide.

Early Years and Hollywood Glamour

Marlene Dietrich began her rise to stardom in the late 1920s and early 1930s, with her breakout role in "The Blue Angel" catapulting her to international fame. Her early style was a unique blend of old-world European glamour and Hollywood sophistication. Dietrich was known for her sultry screen presence and ability to captivate audiences with her exotic looks and alluring charm. Her early wardrobe featured glamorous gowns, luxurious furs, and intricate beadwork which emphasized her statuesque figure and enigmatic allure.

Evolution of Style

Throughout her career, Marlene Dietrich's style evolved into something uniquely her own, characterized by a daring mix of masculine and feminine elements. She was one of the first women in Hollywood to embrace androgyny, often seen in tailored tuxedos, men's suits, and trousers. Dietrich's collaboration with designer Travis Banton resulted in some of her most iconic looks, including the famous tuxedo she wore in "Morocco." Her bold fashion choices challenged societal norms and redefined what it meant to be feminine and glamorous. Over time, her style became synonymous with elegance, sophistication, and a fearless attitude toward fashion.

Casual and Charisma

Marlene Dietrich, off-screen, integrated comfort with sophistication, and was known for her impeccable casual style. Her casual wardrobe often included tailored trousers, crisp white shirts, and perfectly fitted blazers. Dietrich's ability to look effortlessly chic in simple, yet stylish outfits was a testament to her innate sense of style and charisma.

Stylish Ambassador of Elegance

Marlene Dietrich was a stylish ambassador of elegance and sophistication. Her fashion choices were closely followed by fans and critics alike, and she was often featured in fashion magazines and on best-dressed lists. Dietrich's influence on fashion extended beyond her film roles; she was a muse for designers and a trendsetter in the fashion world. Her bold use of menswear-inspired pieces and her penchant for luxurious fabrics and meticulous tailoring set a new standard for elegance and sophistication in fashion.

Legacy of Style

The legacy of Marlene Dietrich as a style icon is enduring and profoundly influential. Her fearless approach to fashion and ability to seamlessly blend masculine and feminine elements continue to inspire modern designers and fashion lovers.

Louise Brooks

Marlene Dietrich

Coco Chanel

Elsa Schiaparelli

Katharine Hepburn

Katharine Hepburn was a legendary actress known for her fierce independence and strong-willed characters. Her distinctive fusion of androgynous elegance and effortless sophistication remains a source of inspiration for fashion enthusiasts.

Early Years and Hollywood Glamour

Katharine Hepburn rose to fame in the 1930s, quickly establishing herself as a leading lady in Hollywood. Unlike many of her contemporaries, Hepburn's early style was characterized by a preference for tailored, practical clothing over the glamorous gowns typical of the era. She often wore trousers, blazers, and collared shirts, which set her apart and showcased her independent spirit. This departure from traditional Hollywood glamour was a bold statement, reflecting her desire to be seen as more than just a glamorous movie star.

Evolution of Style

Katharine Hepburn's style evolved, yet consistently maintained a sense of timeless elegance and individuality. She favored high-waisted trousers, crisp button-down shirts, and blazers, all of which became her signature look. Hepburn's collaboration with costume designer Walter Plunkett resulted in many iconic on-screen looks, including the elegant ensembles in "The Philadelphia Story." Her preference for menswear-inspired fashion was revolutionary, challenging traditional gender norms and paving the way for future generations of women to embrace similar styles.

Casual and Charisma

Off-screen, Katharine Hepburn was known for her impeccable casual style, which seamlessly blended comfort with sophistication. Her everyday wardrobe often included simple yet stylish pieces such as tailored trousers, turtlenecks, and loafers. Hepburn's ability to look effortlessly chic in casual attire was a testament to her innate sense of style and charisma.

Stylish Ambassador of Elegance

Hepburn's influence on fashion extended beyond her film roles; she was a muse for designers and a trendsetter in the fashion world. Her bold embrace of androgynous fashion and her commitment to personal style over fleeting trends set a new standard for elegance and individuality.

Legacy of Style

The legacy of Katharine Hepburn as a style icon is enduring and profoundly influential. Her iconic style, marked by timeless elegance, refined sophistication, and a hint of rebellious spirit, inspires countless generations of fashion enthusiasts.

Lauren Bacall

Lauren Bacall, the legendary actress known for her sultry voice and captivating presence, remains one of the most influential style icons of the 20th century.

Early Years and Hollywood Glamour

Lauren Bacall burst onto the Hollywood scene in the 1940s, quickly establishing herself as a leading lady known for her striking looks and cool demeanor. Her early style was characterized by classic Hollywood glamour, featuring tailored suits, pencil skirts, and elegant gowns. Bacall's signature look often included high-waisted trousers paired with crisp blouses and blazers, reflecting a blend of masculine and feminine elements ahead of its time.

Evolution of Style

Throughout her career, Lauren Bacall's style evolved, yet always maintained a sense of timeless elegance. She favored clean lines, minimalist designs, and high-quality fabrics that exuded sophistication. Bacall's wardrobe was marked by a preference for neutral colors and understated elegance, often accented by bold accessories such as statement jewelry and scarves. Her collaborations with renowned designers like Norman Norell and Yves Saint Laurent helped cement her status as a fashion icon. Bacall's style evolution mirrored her growth as an actress, from the sultry ingenue of "To Have and Have Not" to the sophisticated star of films like "Designing Woman."

Casual and Charisma

Off-screen, Lauren Bacall was known for her impeccable casual style. Her everyday looks often included tailored trousers, simple yet chic blouses, and classic trench coats. Bacall's casual wardrobe also featured timeless pieces like cashmere sweaters, loafers, and oversized sunglasses. Her ability to look effortlessly chic in casual attire was a testament to her innate sense of style and charisma. Bacall's natural elegance and confidence shone through in her off-duty looks, making her a style icon in formal and casual settings.

Stylish Ambassador of Elegance

Lauren Bacall's influence extended beyond her film roles; she was a stylish ambassador of elegance and sophistication. Her impeccable taste and refined style made her a muse for designers and a trendsetter in the fashion world. Her preference for classic, well-tailored clothing sets a standard for elegance that inspires modern fashion.

Legacy of Style

Bacall's ability to seamlessly blend classic Hollywood glamour with modern chic has left a lasting impact on the fashion industry. Exhibitions and retrospectives have celebrated her style, highlighting her influence on fashion over the decades.

Wallis Simpson

Wallis Simpson, the Duchess of Windsor, remains one of the most influential style icons of the 20th century. Her sophisticated and daring fashion choices left a lasting impact on the fashion world.

Early Years and Royal Elegance

Wallis Simpson entered the international spotlight through her relationship with King Edward VIII, which led to his abdication of the throne in 1936 so he could marry her. Early on, her style was marked by a sleek, streamlined elegance that contrasted sharply with the more traditional, conservative fashion of the British royal family. Wallis favored clean lines, tailored silhouettes, and luxurious fabrics, often choosing simple yet striking designs that emphasized her slim figure.

Evolution of Style

Over the years, Wallis Simpson's style evolved to become even more polished and distinctive. She worked closely with some of the most renowned designers of her time, including Hubert de Givenchy, Cristóbal Balenciaga, and Elsa Schiaparelli. Her wardrobe was characterized by impeccably tailored dresses, sharp suits, and exquisite evening gowns. Wallis was known for bold colors, intricate embroidery, and statement jewelry. One of her most famous pieces was the "Lobster Dress" designed by Schiaparelli, which featured a striking lobster motif and was considered avant-garde at the time.

Casual and Charisma

Wallis Simpson was known for her chic and sophisticated casual style. Her off-duty looks often included tailored trousers, elegant blouses, and classic knitwear. She favored monochromatic ensembles and was commonly seen in tailored jackets and pencil skirts which showcased her figure. Wallis's casual style exuded confidence and refinement, whether at leisure in the South of France or attending more relaxed social events.

Stylish Ambassador of Elegance

As an ambassador of style and elegance, Wallis Simpson's influence extended far beyond her wardrobe. She was a muse to many designers and a fixture in the international social scene, where her fashion choices were closely watched and emulated. Wallis's impeccable taste and eye for detail made her a trendsetter, and she was often featured in fashion magazines and society columns. Her preference for couture and bespoke clothing set her apart as a fashion leader.

Legacy of Style

The legacy of Wallis Simpson as a style icon is enduring. Her sophisticated and daring fashion sense inspires modern designers and fashion lovers. Numerous exhibitions, books, and films have been dedicated to her life and style. Wallis's ability to combine elegance with a touch of rebellion has left an indelible mark on the fashion world.

Marilyn Monroe

Marilyn Monroe, the legendary actress and pop culture icon, became one of the most recognized and enduring style figures of the 20th century. Her glamorous and sensual style continues to inspire fashion enthusiasts worldwide.

Early Years and Hollywood Glamour

Marilyn Monroe rose to international fame in the 1950s with her captivating performances in films like "Gentlemen Prefer Blondes" and "Some Like It Hot." Her style during her Hollywood years was characterized by an alluring blend of glamour and sex appeal. Monroe was known for her figure-hugging dresses, plunging necklines, and an array of glamorous gowns that showcased her hourglass figure. One of her most memorable looks was the iconic white halter dress she wore in "The Seven Year Itch," which became one of the most famous images in cinematic history.

Evolution of Style

Marilyn Monroe's style evolved from the early days of her career as she transitioned from a struggling actress to a Hollywood superstar. Initially favoring more conservative looks, Monroe's style became increasingly bold and sophisticated as she gained confidence and recognition. She often collaborated with costume designers like William Travilla, who created some of her most iconic looks. Monroe's wardrobe included glamorous evening gowns, elegant cocktail dresses, and tailored suits, always emphasizing her natural curves.

Lauren Bacall

Katharine Hepburn

Wallis Simpson

Marylin Monroe

Casual and Charisma

Marilyn Monroe was also known for her effortless casual style, which combined comfort with a touch of glamour. Her off-duty looks often included simple yet chic pieces like capri pants, fitted sweaters, and button-down shirts. Monroe's casual style was relaxed and approachable, yet always maintained an element of allure. She often wore high-waisted jeans, ballet flats, and oversized sunglasses, creating a look that was both practical and stylish.

Stylish Pop Culture Icon

As a pop culture icon, Marilyn Monroe's influence on fashion extended beyond her wardrobe. She became a symbol of the Hollywood glamour of the 1950s and an embodiment of the era's beauty ideals. Monroe's impact on fashion and beauty standards was profound. Her iconic status was further cemented by her association with high-profile events and personalities, including her famous performance of "Happy Birthday, Mr. President" in a dazzling, form-fitting gown designed by Jean Louis.

Legacy of Style

Marilyn Monroe's timeless beauty, glamorous fashion choices, and unique blend of sensuality continue to be celebrated and emulated by designers and fashion lovers worldwide. Her talent for seamlessly blending sophistication with an approachable appeal has made a lasting impact on the fashion industry.

Jaqueline Kennedy Onassis

Jacqueline Kennedy Onassis was one of the most influential style icons of the 20th century. She is still admired today for her elegance and sophistication in dress.

Early Years and Royal Elegance

Jackie Kennedy became a fashion icon as soon as she became the First Lady of the United States, following her marriage to John F. Kennedy in 1953. Her early style was characterized by classic, elegant designs that were both modern and subtle. Jackie was known for her love of clean lines, simple colors, and refined details. Her wedding dress, designed by Ann Lowe, was a spectacular example of classic elegance, featuring a lace bodice and a full skirt.

Evolution of Style

Jackie's style evolved, but it always retained her signature simplicity and elegance. During John F. Kennedy's presidency, Jackie became an international fashion icon. Her wardrobe included pieces from top designers like Oleg Cassini, Givenchy, and Chanel. She was known for wearing elegant tweed suits, simple dresses, and classic coats. Her favorite colors were pastels and neutral shades. One of the most iconic elements of her style was her signature pillbox hats and oversized sunglasses, which became her trademark.

Casual and Charisma

Jackie Kennedy was also a master of casual style, which combined comfort with sophistication. Her everyday outfits were simple yet always elegant. Frequently seen in capri pants, elegant sweaters, and ballet flats, Jackie demonstrated that one could look stylish without sacrificing comfort. Her summer outfits, including simple white dresses and espadrilles, epitomized effortless elegance. Jackie was also known for her love of horseback riding, which often influenced her fashion choices, evident in her classic shirts and comfortable trousers.

Stylish Fashion Ambassador

Jackie Kennedy Onassis was not only a fashion icon but also an ambassador of American style to the world. Her influence on fashion was immense, and her fashion choices were widely commented on and emulated. Jackie supported American designers and was a pioneer in promoting American fashion abroad. Her style was elegant yet always thoughtful, making her a role model for many women. Jackie was also known for hosting elegant parties at the White House, where her stylish ensembles always drew attention.

Legacy of Style

The legacy of Jackie Kennedy Onassis as a style icon is immensely influential. Her elegance and fashion sense continue to inspire fashion enthusiasts and designers. Exhibitions dedicated to her style, numerous publications, and tributes from contemporary designers attest to her lasting impact. Jackie was not only a fashion icon but also a symbol of class and sophistication that has stood the test of time.

Grace Kelly

Grace Kelly, the legendary actress and Princess of Monaco, became one of the most iconic style figures of the 20th century. Her sophisticated style inspires fashion enthusiasts worldwide.

Early Years and Hollywood Glamour

Grace Kelly rose to international fame in the 1950s with her captivating performances in films like "Rear Window" and "To Catch a Thief." She was known for her elegant dresses, chic accessories, and impeccable taste. Her preference for classic silhouettes and luxurious fabrics set her apart as a true fashion icon. One of her most memorable looks was the Edith Head-designed gown she wore to the 1955 Academy Awards, where she won the Best Actress Oscar for "The Country Girl."

Evolution of Style

Grace Kelly's style evolved seamlessly from Hollywood star to royalty. After marriage to Prince Rainier III of Monaco in 1956, Kelly's wardrobe reflected her new status as a princess. Her wedding dress, designed by Helen Rose, remains one of the most famous bridal gowns in history, featuring intricate lace, silk taffeta, and a classic silhouette. Kelly's royal wardrobe was marked by elegant evening gowns, tailored suits, and refined accessories. She favored designers such as Christian Dior, Balenciaga, and Yves Saint Laurent, and her style was always marked by a sense of grace and poise.

Casual and Charisma

Grace Kelly was also known for her effortless casual style, which combined comfort with elegance. Her off-duty looks often included chic yet simple pieces like tailored trousers, crisp white shirts, and ballet flats. Kelly popularized the Hermès handbag, later named the "Kelly bag" in her honor. Her casual ensembles often featured timeless staples, such as knit sweaters, silk scarves, and trench coats, all worn with effortless sophistication.

Stylish Ambassador of Royalty

As Princess of Monaco, Grace Kelly became a global ambassador of style and elegance. Her royal appearances were always marked by impeccable fashion choices that balanced tradition with modernity. Kelly's influence extended beyond her wardrobe; she helped to promote Monaco as a glamorous and fashionable destination. Her philanthropic work, including founding the Princess Grace Foundation, was also conducted with the same elegance and dedication brought to her fashion.

Legacy of Style

Grace Kelly's timeless elegance and sophisticated fashion choices continue to be celebrated and emulated by designers and fashion lovers worldwide. Countless exhibitions, books, and films have celebrated her life and style, solidifying her status as an enduring fashion icon. Grace Kelly's ability to seamlessly blend Hollywood glamour with royal refinement has left an indelible mark on the fashion world.

Audrey Hepburn

Audrey Hepburn, the iconic actress and dedicated humanitarian, emerged as one of the most recognizable fashion icons of the 20th century. Her timeless style, characterized by its elegance, simplicity, and sophistication, continues to inspire fashion enthusiasts across the globe. Her influence extends beyond her cinematic achievements, leaving an indelible mark on fashion and grace.

Early Years and Classic Elegance

Audrey Hepburn gained international fame in the 1950s through her unforgettable film roles in "Roman Holiday" and "Breakfast at Tiffany's." Her style, both on and off the screen, was always impeccable. Hepburn introduced minimalist elegance to fashion, characterized by simple yet striking designs. Her iconic black dress designed by Hubert de Givenchy for "Breakfast at Tiffany's" became one of the most recognizable outfits in the history of cinema and fashion.

Evolution of Style

Audrey Hepburn's style evolved while always maintaining simplicity and classicism. Her collaboration with Hubert de Givenchy was crucial to her image. Givenchy created many of her most famous outfits, both on and off the screen. Hepburn led the way in the "little black dress" style, that evolved into an essential element of an elegant wardrobe. Her favorite wardrobe pieces included simple dresses, chic trousers, classic ballet flats, and pearls that emphasized her slender figure and natural elegance.

Casual and Charisma

Audrey Hepburn was also a master of casual style, combining comfort with sophistication. Her everyday outfits, such as simple capri pants, elegant sweaters, and ballet flats, were both practical and stylish. Hepburn often wore white shirts, trench coats, and large sunglasses, which became her trademark. Her natural elegance and effortless style were evident in every outfit, regardless of the occasion.

Stylish Humanitarian Ambassador

Audrey Hepburn was not only a fashion icon but also a dedicated humanitarian. As a UNICEF ambassador, Hepburn visited developing countries to draw attention to children's issues. Her fashion choices during these trips were always carefully considered to show respect and empathy for local cultures. Hepburn was known for simple yet elegant outfits appropriate for such occasions.

Legacy of Style

The legacy of Audrey Hepburn as a style icon is enduring and immensely influential. Her style is continuously emulated by generations of women worldwide. Exhibitions and books dedicated to her fashion, as well as numerous tributes by contemporary designers, attest to her lasting impact. Audrey Hepburn was not only a talented actress but also a model of class and elegance that has stood the test of time.

Brigitte Bardot

Brigitte Bardot, the iconic French actress, singer, and fashion muse, emerged as one of the most recognizable style icons of the 20th century. Her daring and effortless chic sense still captivates and inspires fashion enthusiasts around the globe.

Early Years and Glamorous Beginnings

Brigitte Bardot rose to international fame in the 1950s with her captivating performances in films like "And God Created Woman" and "Contempt." Her style during her early years was characterized by an alluring blend of glamour and femininity. Bardot was known for her tousled hair, sultry makeup, and effortlessly chic outfits. Her preference for body-hugging dresses, plunging necklines, and playful, youthful ensembles set her apart as a true fashion icon. One of her most memorable looks was the gingham wedding dress she wore when she married actor Jacques Charrier in 1959, which sparked a major trend in bridal fashion.

Evolution of Style

Brigitte Bardot's style evolved over the years, always maintaining a sense of effortless elegance and sensuality. As her career progressed, Bardot embraced a more relaxed and bohemian aesthetic. She often wore off-the-shoulder tops, capri pants, and ballet flats, popularizing the casual yet chic "Bardot look." She collaborated with designers like Pierre Balmain and Christian Dior, who created some of her most iconic looks, blending sophistication with a touch of rebellion.

Casual and Charisma

Brigitte Bardot was also known for her effortless casual style, which combined comfort with a touch of glamour. Her off-duty looks often included simple yet chic pieces like high-waisted shorts, oversized sweaters, and wide-brimmed hats. Bardot's casual style was relaxed and approachable, yet always maintained an element of allure. She often wore flat shoes, espadrilles, and denim, creating a look that was both practical and stylish.

Stylish Pop Culture Icon

As a pop culture icon, Brigitte Bardot's influence on fashion extended beyond her wardrobe. She became a symbol of the free-spirited and liberated woman of the 1960s. Bardot inspired countless fashion trends and imitations. Her iconic status was further cemented by her association with high-profile events and personalities, including her appearances at the Cannes Film Festival.

Legacy of Style

Brigitte Bardot's legacy as a style icon remains profoundly impactful. Her timeless beauty, daring fashion sense, and unique mix of sensuality and casual elegance continue to inspire designers and fashion enthusiasts around the globe. Bardot's talent for effortlessly blending glamour with a laid-back attitude has made a lasting impression on the fashion industry.

Audrey Hepburn

Grace Kelly

Brigitte Bardot

Jacqueline Kennedy

Diana, Princess of Wales

Princess Diana, also known as Lady Di, remains one of the most influential style icons of the 20th century. Her elegant yet accessible style evolved, gaining recognition among fashion elites and ordinary people worldwide.

Early Years and Royal Elegance

Diana Spencer entered the global fashion scene upon engagement to Prince Charles in 1981. Initially, her style was more traditional, featuring plenty of ruffles, bows, and classic pastel-colored dresses typical of a young aristocrat of that era. Her wedding gown, designed by David and Elizabeth Emanuel, was a spectacular display of royal extravagance with its long train and billowing sleeves, instantly making her an icon.

Evolution of Style

Over the years, Diana began to experiment with fashion, opting for more modern and daring creations. She collaborated with many renowned designers, including Catherine Walker, Bruce Oldfield, and Gianni Versace. Her style became more refined and elegant, evident in the simple yet striking evening gowns, stylish suits, and chic accessories she chose. One of the most memorable moments was her black silk dress, dubbed the "revenge dress," which she wore to a Serpentine Gallery event in 1994, the same day Prince Charles admitted to infidelity in a televised interview. This dress was a bold expression of Diana's confidence and independence.

Casual and Charisma

Princess Diana was also known for her impeccable casual style. Her everyday outfits were just as inspiring as her formal attire. Often seen in jeans, oversized sweaters, classic blazers, and shirts, she demonstrated an ability to blend elegance with comfort. Her famous sporty outfits, including cycling shorts and sweatshirts, foreshadowed current athleisure fashion trends.

Stylish Ambassador of Humanitarianism

Diana was not only a fashion icon but also an ambassador for many important humanitarian causes. Her fashion choices during charitable trips and meetings with people were always carefully considered to show respect and solidarity. One of the most memorable moments was her visit to Angola in 1997, where she was photographed wearing a protective helmet and vest during a campaign against landmines.

Legacy of Style

Princess Diana remains an enduring source of inspiration for many women, including younger generations. Her sons, Prince William and Prince Harry, and their wives, Kate Middleton and Meghan Markle, often draw on Diana's style in their fashion choices. Exhibitions dedicated to her style and numerous publications continue to celebrate her influence on the fashion world.

Diana Vreeland

Diana Vreeland was the legendary fashion editor and tastemaker. Her visionary approach to fashion and larger-than-life persona left an indelible mark on the industry, inspiring generations of designers, editors, and fashion enthusiasts.

Early Years and Fashion Journalism

Diana Vreeland's journey into fashion began in the 1930s when she started writing a column for Harper's Bazaar titled "Why Don't You...?" Her witty and imaginative suggestions, such as "Why don't you... rinse your blonde child's hair in dead champagne?" captured the readers and showcased her unique perspective on style. Vreeland's early style was characterized by a blend of sophistication and whimsy, often seen in her bold choices of colors, patterns, and accessories. Her ability to transform everyday fashion into extraordinary statements set the tone for her illustrious career in fashion journalism.

Evolution of Style

As the fashion editor at Harper's Bazaar and later as editor-in-chief of Vogue, Vreeland championed a more daring and eclectic approach to fashion. She was known for her impeccable taste and ability to spot and nurture emerging talent. Her wardrobe reflected her adventurous spirit, often featuring vibrant colors, dramatic silhouettes, and luxurious fabrics. Vreeland's collaboration with photographers like Richard Avedon and designers such as Yves Saint Laurent helped shape some of the most iconic fashion images of the 20th century.

Casual and Charisma

Off-duty, Diana Vreeland's style remained as captivating as her editorial work. She had a flair for combining high fashion with personal comfort, often seen in kaftans, statement jewelry, and exotic prints. Vreeland's charismatic personality and love for the extraordinary were evident in her everyday attire.

Stylish Ambassador of Fashion

Diana Vreeland was a key figure in promoting fashion as an art form. Her exhibitions at the Metropolitan Museum of Art's Costume Institute, including "The World of Balenciaga" and "The Glory of Russian Costume," showcased her keen eye for curation and dedication to celebrating fashion history. Her ability to bring fashion to life in such dynamic and educational ways cemented her status as a true style ambassador.

Legacy of Style

Diana Vreeland's visionary approach to fashion editing transformed the industry, setting new standards for creativity and innovation. Her influence continues to be felt through the work of contemporary designers and fashion editors who draw inspiration from her fearless approach to style. Her memoir, "D.V.," and numerous biographies provide insight into her remarkable life and career, further solidifying her legacy. The Diana Vreeland Estate continues to celebrate her contributions to fashion.

Carolina Herrera

Carolina Herrera, the esteemed fashion designer and businesswoman, is celebrated for her timeless elegance and sophisticated style. With a career spanning over four decades, Herrera's influence on fashion is profound, making her a true icon in the industry.

Early Years and Emergence of Signature Style

Carolina Herrera's journey into fashion began in the 1980s when she launched her first collection in New York. Her style became synonymous with classic sophistication. Herrera's early designs featured clean lines, impeccable tailoring, and luxurious fabrics, setting a high standard for modern elegance. Her signature look, often including crisp white blouses paired with dramatic skirts or tailored trousers, became an enduring symbol of her brand.

Evolution of Style

Over the years, Carolina Herrera's style has evolved while maintaining its core principles of elegance and refinement. She is known for her ability to blend traditional elements with contemporary trends, creating timeless pieces that appeal to women of all ages. Herrera's collections frequently feature bold colors, intricate embroidery, and exquisite craftsmanship.

Casual and Charisma

Carolina Herrera's off-duty style is as refined as her formal attire, characterized by effortless elegance and understated luxury. Even in casual settings, she exudes grace and poise, often seen in chic yet comfortable outfits that reflect her sophisticated aesthetic. Herrera's casual wardrobe includes well-fitted jeans, tailored blazers, and simple yet stylish tops, all accessorized with her signature pearls or statement jewelry. Her charisma and natural elegance shine through in her casual looks, making her a timeless style icon on and off the runway.

Stylish Ambassador of Fashion

As the founder and creative director of her eponymous fashion house, Carolina Herrera has become a global ambassador for elegance and sophistication. Her designs are worn by some of the most influential women in the world, including First Ladies, celebrities, and royalty. Herrera's presence at fashion events and involvement in philanthropic activities further solidified her status as a leading figure in the fashion world.

Legacy of Style

Carolina Herrera's legacy as a style icon is characterized by her unwavering commitment to elegance, quality, and timeless design. Her influence on fashion is far-reaching, with her designs continuing to inspire and captivate new generations of fashion enthusiasts. Herrera's ability to create pieces that transcend trends and remain relevant over time is a testament to her extraordinary talent and vision. Her timeless elegance and sophisticated style inspire fashion lovers.

Queen Rania of Jordan

Queen Rania al-Abdullah of Jordan is celebrated not only for her humanitarian efforts and advocacy work but also for her impeccable sense of style. As a modern queen, she seamlessly blends traditional and contemporary fashion, becoming a global style icon admired for her elegance and grace.

Early Years and Emergence of Signature Style

Queen Rania's journey into the public eye began when she married King Abdullah II of Jordan in 1993. From the outset, her style was marked by a blend of modesty and modernity, reflecting her royal status and progressive outlook. Her early appearances showcased a sophisticated and polished aesthetic, often incorporating traditional Jordanian elements with a contemporary twist. Queen Rania's ability to balance cultural respect with modern fashion set her apart as a unique and influential figure in the fashion world.

Evolution of Style

Queen Rania's style has evolved, consistently reflecting her role as a global ambassador for Jordan and a champion of women's rights. She is known for her preference for clean lines, tailored silhouettes, and elegant designs that convey authority and femininity. Queen Rania often wears creations by renowned international designers such as Elie Saab, Valentino, and Giorgio Armani, as well as supporting local Jordanian designers.

Princess Diana

Carolina Herrera

Queen Rania

Diana Vreeland

Casual and Charisma

Queen Rania's off-duty style is equally impressive, characterized by its effortless chic and understated luxury. Her casual wardrobe often includes well-fitted jeans, elegant blouses, and classic blazers, reflecting her modern and practical approach to fashion. She is frequently seen in stylish yet comfortable outfits appropriate for her engagements and travels.

Stylish Ambassador of Humanitarianism

As a prominent global figure, Queen Rania uses her platform to advocate for education, health, and women's empowerment. Her fashion choices often reflect her commitment to these causes, with a focus on ethical and sustainable fashion. She is known for wearing pieces that promote local artisans and designers, showcasing Jordan's rich cultural heritage on the world stage. Queen Rania's stylish yet thoughtful approach to fashion serves as an extension of her humanitarian work, demonstrating that style and substance can go hand in hand.

Legacy of Style

Queen Rania's legacy as a style icon is characterized by her ability to blend tradition with modernity, creating a distinctive and influential fashion narrative. Her elegant and refined fashion choices continue to inspire women. Queen Rania's influence extends beyond fashion, as she continues to advocate for important social issues and inspire positive change through her work and personal example.

Sheikha Moza bint Nasser

Sheikha Moza bint Nasser of Qatar is renowned for her elegance, sophistication, and visionary contributions to education and social causes. As a global fashion icon, she masterfully blends traditional Qatari elements with contemporary haute couture, making a profound statement on the world stage.

Early Years and Emergence of Signature Style

Sheikha Moza first captured international attention with her refined and elegant fashion. From the outset, her style has been characterized by a seamless integration of modesty and high fashion, respecting her cultural heritage while embracing modern design. Her early public appearances showcased a sophisticated and polished aesthetic, often featuring luxurious fabrics and exquisite tailoring. Sheikha Moza's ability to balance traditional and contemporary styles quickly set her apart as a unique and influential figure in the fashion world.

Evolution of Style

Over the years, Sheikha Moza's style has evolved, reflecting her roles as a mother, philanthropist, and global ambassador for Qatar. Her wardrobe features a mix of traditional abayas and turbans with high-end designer pieces from Valentino, Jean Paul Gaultier, and Chanel. She often chooses bold colors, intricate embroidery, and modern silhouettes, demonstrating her confidence and fashion-forward thinking. Her evolution in style is marked by consistent elegance and sophistication, showcasing her ability to adapt to various settings and occasions while maintaining her distinctive look.

Casual and Charisma

Even in casual settings, Sheikha Moza exudes effortless elegance and charisma. Her everyday style often includes tailored trousers, stylish blouses, and chic accessories, reflecting her modern and practical approach to fashion. Sheikha Moza is known for her impeccable taste and attention to detail, evident in her casual wardrobe choices.

Stylish Ambassador of Humanitarianism

Sheikha Moza is not only a fashion icon but also a dedicated humanitarian and advocate for education and social development. Her fashion choices often reflect her commitment to these causes, with a focus on ethical and sustainable fashion. She frequently supports designers who promote social responsibility and sustainability, aligning her fashion choices with philanthropic values. Sheikha Moza's stylish yet thoughtful approach to fashion serves as an extension of her humanitarian work, demonstrating that elegance and substance can coexist.

Legacy of Style

Sheikha Moza's legacy as a style icon is her ability to blend tradition with modernity, creating a unique and influential fashion narrative. Her influence extends beyond fashion, as she continues to advocate for social issues and inspire positive change through her work and personal example.

Catherine, Princess of Wales

Catherine, Princess of Wales, has become one of the most influential style icons of the 21st century. Her fashion choices are closely followed and admired, reflecting a perfect blend of modern elegance, regal poise, and accessibility.

Early Years and Emergence of Signature Style

Kate Middleton's style began to attract significant attention when she started dating Prince William. Her early fashion choices were characterized by casual chic and classic elegance, often incorporating high-street fashion with a touch of luxury. Her engagement announcement in 2010, where she wore a stunning blue Issa dress, marked the beginning of her influence on global fashion. This dress sold out within hours, illustrating her immediate impact on fashion trends.

Evolution of Style

Since becoming the Duchess of Cambridge, Kate Middleton's style has developed to encompass a more sophisticated and polished aesthetic while maintaining her accessible charm. She seamlessly combines high-end designer pieces from brands like Alexander McQueen, Jenny Packham, and Catherine Walker with affordable items from labels such as Zara and L.K. Bennett. Her wardrobe includes timeless coats, elegant dresses, and tailored suits, all chosen with impeccable taste. Notable moments include her wedding dress, designed by Sarah

Burton for Alexander McQueen, which became an instant classic and inspired bridal fashion worldwide.

Casual and Charisma

Even in her casual attire, Catherine, Princess of Wales, exudes elegance and approachability. Her off-duty looks often include well-fitted jeans, Breton striped tops, and practical yet stylish outerwear. She is frequently seen in casual but chic outfits during public engagements and outdoor activities, often pairing simple pieces with statement accessories.

Stylish Ambassador of Royal Duties

As a senior member of the British royal family, Princess Catherine uses her fashion choices to convey respect and diplomacy during official engagements. She often selects outfits that pay homage to the host country's culture and traditions, showcasing her thoughtfulness and attention to detail. Her fashion diplomacy was evident during her tours of Canada, India, and Pakistan, where she wore garments by local designers and incorporated traditional elements into her wardrobe.

Legacy of Style

Princess Catherine's legacy as a style icon is firmly established through her influence on fashion trends and her ability to make classic, elegant fashion accessible to a broad audience. Her consistent and timeless approach to style has led to numerous fashion blogs and social media accounts dedicated to chronicling her outfits.

Victoria Beckham

Victoria Beckham has transformed from a pop star into a renowned fashion designer and style icon. Her evolution in the fashion world has been marked by a distinct blend of sophistication, minimalism, and modern elegance, earning her a place among the most influential fashion figures of the 21st century.

Early Years and Emergence of Signature Style

Victoria Beckham first entered the global spotlight as "Posh Spice" in the iconic girl group, the Spice Girls. Her early style was characterized by bold, edgy, and glamorous looks, befitting her pop star persona. From mini dresses to platform shoes, Victoria's fashion choices during this era were daring and trendsetting. As she transitioned from music to fashion, her style evolved into something more refined and sophisticated, reflecting her growing interest in high fashion.

Evolution of Style

Victoria Beckham's style has evolved significantly since her Spice Girls days. As she established herself as a serious fashion designer, her style became more minimalist and elegant. She is known for her sleek, tailored silhouettes, often favoring monochromatic palettes and clean lines. Victoria's designs, under her eponymous fashion label launched in 2008, reflect this aesthetic, featuring structured dresses, elegant separates, and timeless pieces that exude confidence and sophistication.

Casual and Charisma

Even in her casual attire, Victoria Beckham maintains an air of effortless chic. She often opts for well-fitted jeans, simple tees, and impeccably tailored blazers, accessorized with oversized sunglasses and statement handbags. Her casual looks are practical and stylish, showcasing her knack for elevating everyday fashion.

Stylish Ambassador of Fashion and Business

Victoria Beckham is not only a style icon but also a successful businesswoman and fashion ambassador. Her transition from pop star to fashion mogul has been marked by a series of critically acclaimed collections that have garnered respect within the industry. She often attends major fashion events and is seen wearing her designs, embodying the brand's ethos of modern elegance and empowerment. Victoria's influence extends beyond her style; she has become a role model for aspiring designers and businesswomen, demonstrating that reinvention and success in multiple fields are possible.

Legacy of Style

Victoria Beckham's legacy as a style icon is characterized by her sophisticated aesthetic and impact on modern fashion. Her fashion label continues to thrive, known for its luxurious yet wearable designs. The "VB effect" is evident in the way her style inspires women around the world to embrace sleek, elegant fashion. Victoria's contributions to the fashion industry are celebrated through accolades and featured in prominent fashion publications.

Princess Catherine

Moza bint Nasser

Victoria Beckham

Carla Bruni-Sarkozy

Carla Bruni-Sarkozy

Carla Bruni-Sarkozy, the Italian-French singer, songwriter, model, and former First Lady of France is renowned for her timeless elegance and sophisticated style. Her fashion evolution, from supermodel to a prominent public figure, showcases a blend of classic chic and modern refinement.

Early Years and Emergence of Signature Style

Carla Bruni began her career as a model in the late 1980s and quickly rose to fame, gracing the covers of prestigious fashion magazines and walking the runways for top designers like Chanel, Versace, and Dior. During her modeling years, her style was characterized by high fashion glamour and versatility, effortlessly transitioning from haute couture gowns to casual chic ensembles.

Evolution of Style

As Carla transitioned from modeling to music and public life, her style evolved into a more sophisticated and polished look. She embraced a classic French aesthetic, favoring tailored suits, elegant dresses, and understated yet luxurious fabrics. Her wardrobe includes timeless pieces like little black dresses, perfectly cut blazers, and chic trench coats. Carla's color palette leans towards neutrals, blacks, and soft pastels, reflecting her preference for simplicity and elegance. Her style evolution is marked by a consistent embrace of timeless fashion, blending contemporary trends with classic silhouettes.

Casual and Charisma

Even in casual settings, Carla Bruni exudes an effortless elegance that is both approachable and chic. She often opts for well-fitted jeans, crisp white shirts, and cashmere sweaters, accessorized with minimal jewelry and classic handbags. Her casual style is a testament to her ability to maintain a polished look without sacrificing comfort.

Stylish Ambassador and First Lady

As the First Lady of France from 2008 to 2012, Carla Bruni-Sarkozy became an ambassador of French elegance and sophistication on the global stage. Her public appearances were marked by impeccably chosen outfits that balanced formality with a modern touch. She often collaborated with renowned designers such as Christian Dior and Yves Saint Laurent for her official wardrobe, reflecting her commitment to promoting French fashion. Carla's role as First Lady further solidified her status as a style icon, with her fashion choices being closely followed and admired worldwide.

Legacy of Style

Carla Bruni's legacy as a style icon is characterized by her enduring elegance and refined taste. Her influence extends beyond her modeling and public life, inspiring fashion enthusiasts and designers with her timeless approach to style. Carla's ability to seamlessly blend classic and contemporary elements continues to resonate with those who appreciate understated elegance and timeless fashion.

Style Questionnaire

1. What does personal style mean to you? What role does it play in your life?

- Describe your understanding of personal style.
- How important is style to you in your daily life?
- How do you feel your style reflects your personality?
- Do you think your style has evolved over the years? How so?

2. Which clothing style do you like the most? Which style best suits the method you live, work, and spend your free time? Does it include elements from any iconic styles described in Chapter IV?

- Identify your favorite clothing style(s) and why you are attracted to them.
- Consider how your preferred style aligns with your daily activities and lifestyle.
- Reflect on the iconic styles mentioned in Chapter IV. Are there specific elements that you incorporate into your style?
- How do you balance comfort and aesthetics in your wardrobe choices?

3. Which person do you particularly admire for their style of dressing? Do you like the style of any elegance icon described in Chapter VI? Can you imagine yourself wearing similar outfits?

- Think about women whose style you admire.

- Describe what aspects of their style appeal to you.

- Reflect on the elegance icons from Chapter VI. Whose style resonates with you the most?

- How would you adapt their style to fit your wardrobe and lifestyle?

4. How can you develop your taste in fashion? What ideas do you have for broadening your horizons in this area? Which methods described in Chapter II can you start implementing?

- Discuss ways to refine and develop your fashion sense.

- List specific activities or practices that could help you enhance your style (e.g., reading fashion magazines, attending fashion shows, following style blogs).

- From the methods outlined in Chapter II, which ones do you find most applicable to your situation?

- How can you keep your fashion sense evolving and stay inspired?

5. What body shape do you have? What types of clothing suit you best? Do you need additional wardrobe pieces to complement your closet based on your body shape? Would you like to add more colors to your wardrobe? What are your thoughts on this?

- Identify your body shape and the types of clothing that flatter it.

- Evaluate your current wardrobe and determine if there are any gaps.

- Consider if you need additional pieces to enhance your wardrobe's versatility and suitability for your body shape.

- Reflect on your wardrobe's color palette. Are there any colors you would like to add? Why?

- How do you plan to integrate new pieces and colors into your wardrobe?

Reflecting on these questions can help you understand your style and how to cultivate it further. Use this questionnaire to explore your fashion preferences, identify areas for growth, and ultimately, create a wardrobe that truly represents you.

List of Illustrations

p. 25, 29, 31: Images from Wikimedia.org.

p. 33: Photos by Laura Merano, © 2024.

p. 35: Images from Wikimedia.org, Unsplash.com. Moodboard by Laura Merano, © 2024.

p. 44, 45, 46, 47, 49, 50, 51, 52, 54, 55, 56: Images from Pixabay.com, Unsplash.com.

p. 59, 61, 63, 65, 67: Packshots by Molton, press materials; Khaki.pl.

p. 71, 75, 79, 83, 87, 91, 95, 99: Images from Pixabay.com, Unsplash.com,Wikimedia.org. Moodboards by Laura Merano, © 2024.

p. 73: Packshots by Molton, press materials; Khaki.pl. Photo in the top right corner: Monnari, press materials, Tweed.pl. Photo in the bottom left corner: Bialcon, press materials, Tweed.pl. Photo in the center: Ochnik, press materials, Tweed.pl.

p. 77: Packshots by Molton, press materials; Khaki.pl. Photos by Wolczanka, press materials, Vrg.pl.

p. 81: Packshots by Molton, press materials; Khaki.pl. Photo in the top right corner: Monnari, press materials, Tweed.pl. Photos in the bottom left corner and in the center: Bialcon, press materials, Tweed.pl.

p. 85: Packshots by Molton, press materials; Khaki.pl. Photo in the center: Greenpoint, press materials, Tweed.pl. Photo in the bottom left corner: Bialcon, press materials, Tweed.pl.

p. 89: Packshots by Molton, press materials; Khaki.pl. Photos by Wolczanka, press materials, Vrg.pl.

p. 93: Packshots by Molton, press materials; Khaki.pl. Photos in the top right corner and in the center: Monnari, press materials, Tweed.pl. Photo in the bottom left corner: Bialcon, press materials, Tweed.pl.

p. 97: Packshots by Molton, press materials; Khaki.pl. Photos in the top right and in the bottom left corner: Monnari, press materials, Tweed.pl. Photo in the center: Bialcon, press materials, Tweed.pl.

p. 101: Packshots by Molton, press materials; Khaki.pl. Photo in the top right corner: Pixabay.com. Photo in the bottom left corner: by Wolczanka, press materials, Vrg.pl. Photo in the center: Greenpoint, press materials, Tweed.pl.

p. 109, 110, 129: Illustrations by Laura Merano, © 2024.

p. 141, 149, 159, 167, 175: Images from Wikimedia.org.

Other Books by Laura Merano

69 Secrets
of Classic Elegance

A Guide to Looking
Your Best Every Day

Illustrated with 150 Colorful Examples
Laura Merano

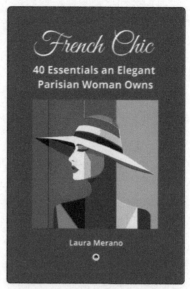

French Chic

40 Essentials an Elegant
Parisian Woman Owns

Laura Merano

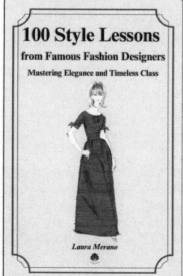

100 Style Lessons
from Famous Fashion Designers
Mastering Elegance and Timeless Class

Laura Merano

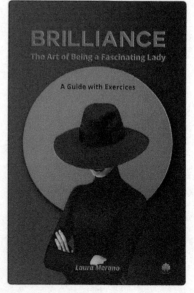

BRILLIANCE
The Art of Being a Fascinating Lady

A Guide with Exercices

Laura Merano

Coquille Dorée

Made in United States
Orlando, FL
15 November 2024

53897113R00104